# You're from *Where*?

By

Gayle Carline

Cover art by Joe Felipe of Market Me
(www.marketme.us).



ISBN: 1943654026
ISBN-13: 978-1-943654-02-4

Published in USA by Dancing Corgi Press

# DEDICATION

To Placentia, and all its lovely people

# ACKNOWLEDGMENTS

Thank you to Heather McRae and the Placentia News-Times for publishing my weekly musings.

Thank you to my husband Dale and our son Marcus for letting me talk about them in my weekly musings.

Thank you to the schools and organizations of Placentia, from Valencia High School, to the Placentia Library, to the Rotary and Women's clubs, for including me and my family. We value our time with you.

And most of all, thank you to the citizens of Placentia who read my musings and tell me how much they love them—or even how much they hate them.

I love you all.

# CONTENTS

The accidental resident ..... 1
Our pearl ..... 3
Placentia, the land of the lost ..... 5
Gracious, if young, guests ..... 8
The midpoint of middle school ..... 12
Obeying all the rules (in my own special way) 15
Valencia High School—so it begins ..... 18
Sometimes the road is bumpy ..... 21
CSI: Placentia ..... 23
When trying to be helpful backfires ..... 26
Living wild in the city ..... 29
Keeping abreast of the news ..... 32
Pomp and circumstance, circumstance and pomp ..... 35
Summer school at El Dorado ..... 38
Making friends with the neighbors ..... 41
Car washing and people watching ..... 44
Fundraising to support our schools ..... 47

A VALENTINE ROMANCE IN PLACENTIA ....................50

SWINGIN' WITH THE PARKS AND REC DEPARTMENT .53

A LITTLE VOLUNTEER WORK AT THE LIBRARY...........56

PLACENTIA NOIR? ..................................................59

A GREAT WAY TO DISCOVER OUR PAST ....................62

FUN AND FUNDRAISING WITH AUTHORS ....................65

SHARING BIG NEWS WITH MY LITTLE CITY..................68

IN PLACENTIA, WE LOVE TO READ ...........................71

WHEN YOUR NEW TOWN BECOMES YOUR HOME TOWN ...................................................................................74

A LITTLE LIBRARY LOVE ..........................................77

MY FIRST PLACENTIA LOVE LETTER ........................80

LISTEN TO THE MUSIC ............................................83

IN PLACENTIA, ONE THING LEADS TO ANOTHER ........86

OF HERITAGES AND REMEMBRANCES ......................89

HERE SHE IS… .......................................................92

I CAN'T SAY NO TO MY CITY......................................95

JUDGING VALENCIA'S TALENT IS NOT EASY .............98

MY TURN AT THE AUTHOR'S LUNCHEON HELM .........101

THE HIGH PRICE OF WANDERING ...........................104

COWABUNGA! WHAT A LOT OF CRABS! ...................107

WHEN TRAGEDY HITS ONE SMALL TOWN, IT HITS US ALL ..........110

EVEN CELEBRITIES KNOW US..........113

GRADUATING FROM TEEN TO QUEEN..........116

PARDON MY FANGIRL MOMENT..........119

ROTARY CLUB IS A GREAT PLACE FOR STUDENTS..........122

CONSTRUCTING LEMONADE OUT OF ROADWORK LEMONS ..........125

ADVICE FOR EVERYONE, EVEN MYSELF..........128

SHOWING THAT LOVIN' FEELING FOR PLACENTIA..........131

MEASURING THE SIZE OF A SMALL TOWN..........134

HONORING A LIFE WELL LIVED..........137

PARADING MY HERITAGE..........140

SAYING GOODBYE..........143

I LOVE A PARADE, AND A CITY..........146

WHEN IT COMES TO PUBLIC SPEAKING, CALL ME CRAZY ..........149

OUR RECREATION IS GOING TO THE DOGS..........152

MAKING PLANS DOESN'T ALWAYS GET THINGS DONE..........155

LEAVE THE PLANNING TO THE EXPERTS..........158

SAYING GOODBYE IN OUR OWN WAY..........161

Construction doesn't always stick to the schedule ....................164

Asking the right questions today to prepare for tomorrow ....................167

Shopping locally has its perks ....................170

Honoring our city is a yearly event ....................173

A life of service, worth remembering ....................176

Serving my community, one task at a time ....................179

There's always an opportunity to volunteer .182

Cultivating a passion for writing is my passion ....................185

Good health requires a little work ....................188

Strolling down memory lane with the Placentia Quarterly ....................191

Walking to the beat is more fun with friends .194

About the Author ....................198

Also by this Author ....................199

## THE ACCIDENTAL RESIDENT

I never meant to move to Placentia, California. When I came to the West Coast to work as a software engineer in 1978, I moved to "Orange County." What I didn't realize was that I'd have to actually live in a city.

I bounced around a few towns until 1984, when I moved to The Pleasant Place. Since then, I've moved twice. Twice I've looked at neighboring towns. Twice I've found what I was looking for in Placentia.

In 2005, I began writing a weekly humor column for the Placentia News-Times, the local paper that is affiliated with the Orange County Register. My columns are a slice-of-life look at an average woman who is a wife, mother, homeowner, and city resident—in other words, me.

For the record, Placentia is pronounced Plah-SEN-cha. We have about 50,000 residents living in 6.6 square miles in north Orange County. We have a hospital, a library, a country club, and our downtown, called Placita Santa Fe boasts some of the best Mexican restaurants in O.C.

As of this publication, I've been writing my column for 10 years. I'll keep writing until they kick me out the door. As much as I enjoy the writing, I enjoy hearing from other Placentia (or P-Town) folks more, especially when they tell me that they identify with whatever I went through.

You'll find this collection is centered on the schools my son attended, the library where I volunteer my time, and various philanthropic organizations where I have been generously invited to speak. There are also a few essays about specific people whom we have loved and lost as a community.

If you are from P-Town, I hope they resonate with your experiences. If you're not familiar with our little city, I hope they inspire you to find what is special about your own town.

I may have landed in P-Town accidentally, but it's where I belong.

*Note: A few of these essays are also included in my first two books, WHAT WOULD ERMA DO, and ARE YOU THERE, ERMA? IT'S ME, GAYLE. I've included them here because they are all about Placentia.*

## OUR PEARL

I just returned from a trip to Santa Barbara, and all I can say is, "How do I love thee, Placentia? Let me count the ways!" (Thanks, Elizabeth Barrett Browning.)

Santa Barbara may be full of beautiful homes on oceanfront property, but you pay for the privilege. I glanced through the real estate section of one of their newspapers and saw one ad for a house that was under $1 million. It was a condo for $750,000, described as a "fixer-upper." If that sounds reasonable to you, you've got too much money.

I think Placentia is lovely, even without a beach. I like to walk my dog down past the Civic Center and stroll the shaded, winding walkways of Chapman Avenue. Bradford House sits so tall and regal on her manicured lawn that I must look at her when I drive by. And the Wagner House beckons me to put on a pretty dress and visit for tea.

Skimming the Santa Barbara weekly paper, I noticed that it was a fancy, stapled and glossy magazine. But it wasn't full of information about their local schools or profiles of their community helpers and heroes. The articles were about the latest fashions and interviews with famous people. And the advertisements were mostly about how to transcend the latest fashion and fame by using various spiritual methods to center your chi and balance your life force.

Frankly, I'd rather know how to balance my checkbook.

In Placentia, our weekly newspaper tells us what our city is doing, from our schools to our roads to all of the people who volunteer to make it work. There are plenty of ads for our local churches, temples and synagogues, and advisors to help us along our spiritual voyage; but we also get information about how to be better parents and neighbors.

I don't blame the Santa Barbara paper for giving their readers what they want. I'm just saying that I don't think I fit into their demographic.

On my last morning, I stopped at a Starbucks for some coffee. It looked just my local shop, but the atmosphere couldn't have been more different. Where I usually see parents and business folks rushing for their morning caffeine, I was drowning in a sea of spoiled twenty-somethings. As I waited in the long line, one of the cashiers began teasing the girl behind me about her new BMW, saying that she thought it was a Honda. Then she proceeded to bypass me and serve her friend.

I may have entered the store wanting a cup of coffee, but I left feeling like I needed a stiff drink. Instead, I pointed my minivan south on the 101 and headed back.

Placentia has been my home for over 20 years, and I like it. I like its tranquility, its proximity to shopping and freeways, and its overall friendliness. Santa Barbara may sparkle like a jewel, but Placentia is the oyster that you open to find a pearl inside.

# PLACENTIA, THE LAND OF THE LOST

Do service companies and delivery men try to make everyone miserable, or is it just me? I have never been the first person on their route. I know that if I am given a window of 8 to 12 in the morning, that they will arrive at 12:15. Or they will call me at noon to tell me that they'll be at my house at 2 p.m… tomorrow… if they come at all.

Even if I call the companies who specify a "Placentia" phone number, my house seems to be off of their beaten path. They act like they need a passport to get to Kraemer and Alta Vista.

It was a Saturday afternoon when my hubby told me that the pilot light on the water heater would not stay lit. I called the service company, who said that they would send someone between 2 and 4 p.m. the next day.

Rearranging my schedule, I was home by 2 p.m., waiting for the service man. At 2:30, our friends called to invite us to go bowling at Concourse and then have dinner at Buca di Beppo. I sent my family along, planning to join them when the service man had left.

At 4 p.m., I called the company. They said the technician had been held up and wouldn't be at my house until 5 p.m. A black cloud began to form over my unwashed head. At 5:30, my hubby Dale called to say they were at the restaurant and how was the heater coming? The cloud grew darker. I called the company again. This time I was told that a technician had called in sick, they were juggling his appointments and didn't have anyone to send to my house. I wasn't on anyone's "normal route," as if Placentia was on Gilligan's Island.

The cloud now took shape of a mushroom.

The man cooed excuses to me, asking if I could wait until tomorrow. "What other option are you offering?" I asked. There was a guttural noise on the line, the sound of brain cells trying to activate. I considered canceling this company and calling another, but if another company treated me this way, I could be four days without a hot shower. After two days, I was already feeling like I lived in my van with a year's newspapers and a small poodle. Sighing, I caved.

"Okay, I guess I'll have to wait until tomorrow," I huffed.

Gleefully, he asked, "Do you want to just keep the same appointment time tomorrow?"

What a dolt.

"Ex-Cuse me?" I hissed. "When do I get to be your priority?"

"You ARE my priority," he assured me.

"I don't think so. You've wasted my afternoon, kept me from going out with my family, and didn't even call me to say that you aren't coming. I think that tomorrow, you're going to make someone else wait while you fix my water heater first thing in the morning."

"But your house isn't on the morning route," he reasoned, as if that was logical to a woman who needs a shower.

"Know what? Not very sympathetic to the whole 'route' thing," I snapped.

Finally, he surrendered. "All right, ma'am," he grumbled as if I was somehow to blame for this mess. "We'll send someone between 8 and 10."

"Thank you," I said crisply, and hung up. Cleaning myself up as much as possible, I raced to the restaurant to meet everyone and share my troubles over a big glass of wine.

The following morning, a very nice technician showed up and fixed the heater for $200. In just a couple of hours, hot water and my sanity were restored.

I'd like to say that I learned something valuable from this experience, and that I'll never let another service company jerk me around, but I know the next time something breaks, someone is out there waiting to play with me like a cat torments a mouse. All I really discovered is that meeting friends and family at a restaurant to eat, drink and kvetch can make life bearable.

## GRACIOUS, IF YOUNG, GUESTS

I recently accompanied my son, Marcus, on a field trip with his 7th grade Kraemer Middle School classmates to San Francisco for a day. The tour included the Bay Model to learn about the importance of water conservation, the Exploratorium to test physical laws with hands-on experiments and Alcatraz Island to learn what happens when good children go bad. These events were sandwiched between two airline flights and lunch on Pier 39.

Mrs. Goodding, the science teacher, obviously had previous experience with this trip. There were plenty of teachers and parents who kept the kids corralled and tour guides who kept us on schedule. My job was to supervise five of the 78 children and, I suppose, keep Placentia's good name intact. How did we do? Well…

The teachers kept saying that, overall, the kids "weren't too bad". It's true, no one was kicked out of the exhibits, no one fell off of the ferry to Alcatraz and the sky marshals did not take any of our group into custody at the airport, so if that's your definition of "not too bad", I guess we met expectations. I can't say that my expectations were higher, but since these were GATE kids, my expectations were different. And wrong.

For example, I expected at least brief moments of calm throughout the day. What I found was a percentage of children who do not rest until their heads hit their pillows and are perky beyond all reason until that happens. When we left for the airport at 4:15 a.m., these kids were making noise. I can't describe it as talking. There were girlish squeals, boyish guffaws, the occasional, "Ah, man!" and "Cut it out", but no discernable sentences. This wall of sound continued on the plane, hummed along at a lower decibel for the tours, then built back up for the trip home. Our plane home was delayed three hours, but the long wait at the airport only recharged their batteries. My ears were still ringing when I collapsed into bed at two in the morning.

I also expected these bright kids to be bright about everything. I should have known better on this one. There are lots of smart people who can find countries on a map yet cannot follow directions. As we pulled up to the Golden Gate Bridge vista point, our tour guide explained that this was where we would stop and take pictures, and pointed out the restrooms to our left. Her words were still hanging in the air, like a comic strip balloon, when a young girl in the back of the bus asked, "Where are we now? Are there restrooms here?" In a sitcom, she would have been the ditzy neighbor, but I know that she can identify mitochondria on a diagram. Ditzy? No, she's just a young girl with many layers.

Likewise incorrect was my assumption that these high-functioning students would huddle around each exhibit and soak in every word from every tour guide. Most of them did stand dutifully around the guides and listen to what was being said. But on the fringes of this core group were the wanderers, whispering to each other and playing with their cell phones.

The impression I got was of kids who, while not acting up, were just not into learning. This did not match what I knew about their academic achievements.

I kept asking Marcus and the teachers, “Are you sure these are all GATE students?”

One of the teachers laughed and said, “Sometimes I think that’s part of the problem.” Thinking about this, I decided she was right. On the one hand, we assume that because these youngsters are smart, they are somehow “above” acting like preteens and should behave like mini-adults. On the other hand, we make allowances for fringe behavior because they’re so darn sharp.

I was still focused on the noise and my expectations as I shared our adventure with my husband at dinner the next evening. I was apparently in exaggeration high gear when Marcus asked, “Was there anything you liked about the trip?”

Hmm. I guess I liked that there was a percentage of kids who listened and learned, and that all of the kids were respectful of others. I liked seeing that my son and his friends were in the core group. And even if I am now an official curmudgeon, I liked remembering my own 7$^{th}$ grade field trips and how I was mostly part of that group, too… with just a hint of acting like the fringe element when the teachers weren’t watching.

So I think we left San Francisco with an image of Placentia as just a normal town with normal kids; preteens trying to rise to an occasion while mapping their own course through life. I hope the "City by the Bay" watched our pilgrimage with a shrug of her shoulders and nod of her head, approving our attempts to raise good kids and the kids' attempts to be good without us.

## THE MIDPOINT OF MIDDLE SCHOOL

Our son, Marcus, has just completed seventh grade at Kraemer Middle School and boy, are we tired. Having come from the homey setting of Morse Elementary School, I'd like to tell incoming seventh graders and their parents:

Don't go, it's a trap.

Seriously, I know that children must go to middle school and they survive it, but I don't know how parents do. I feel like getting a T-shirt that says, "My son went to seventh grade and all I got was this lousy headache." But I do have advice for both the parents and the kids.

For the children, I must warn you that there is no way to prepare you for the shock of having seven teachers with one subject after years of having one teacher with seven subjects. Pat Souto and Robin Mackie did their best with our little sixth graders at Morse, but they simply cannot assign the amount of homework that middle school teachers can.

They would be insane to try to grade it all.

I know we've been trying to get our kids to do their own work and be more independent, but my advice to new seventh graders is to toss all of that independence aside for a year and get your parents involved. Let them know what your homework is each day and let them help you organize it and keep you on track. Don't wait until nine o'clock the night before a project is due to ask them for poster board and pictures from last year's vacation.

Not unless you can afford to pay for their tranquilizers with your allowance.

And a social side note to all of the middle school girls: if you keep telling boys that they dance funny at the school dances at Kraemer, you will not have any dance partners when you get to Valencia High School and beyond.

Encouraging them to dance now means you won't have to sit unhappily at wedding receptions wishing your husband would waltz you around the floor just once.

For the parents, I would just like to let you know that you will never truly be on top of your child's progress in seventh grade. Not unless you are at school every day, talking to every teacher about every assignment. You can read your child's planner to see what homework is due, but you are relying on your child to have written everything down. You can review your child's homework to ensure that it is correct, but you won't know whether it is handed in.

Not until progress reports come out.

So be prepared for the mornings when your child tells you that they ran out of lined paper and couldn't finish last night's assignment. Don't be shocked when you ask them when that big project is due and they say, "I'm not sure." As a matter of fact, you will hear those three words often, as an answer to whether they turned in their report, why they got a low grade on a test, and where they left their gym clothes.

The trip from elementary school to middle school seems like a leap across a chasm. Elementary school held Marcus' hand and steered him through his education; middle school shook him loose and shoved him, unsupervised, into academia. If he could walk in ten minutes late with a cup of coffee, it would be just like going to college. But he'll get through it, probably better than I will.

In the meantime, we have the summer to relax, regroup and renew. Eighth grade, here we come.

## OBEYING ALL THE RULES (IN MY OWN SPECIAL WAY)

I'd like to start this column by telling all of the fine policemen in Placentia that I try hard to obey all of our traffic laws, especially the speed limits. It's my foot that thinks of them more as guidelines…

When I used to drive a Honda Prelude (in Ticket-Me Red), I admittedly liked to punch the accelerator as I shifted manually up the gears. I never got a ticket in that car, but I deserved many.

Now that I drive a minivan, my driving habits have changed. For one thing, it just seems wrong to lay rubber in a "momcar". Plus, it looks stupid. And with today's gas prices, I try to wring every last tenth of a mile out of each gallon I buy. But I still find myself going fast.

I realize that the speed limit down Kraemer Boulevard is forty miles per hour, and I try to be good. But I'm an arrival gal; I just want to get from point A to point B. If there's no traffic, my van tends to drift to a slightly higher "natural" speed of fifty. I know it's wrong, but it feels so right.

My son, Marcus, has been on my case about this since he was old enough to recognize numbers. "How fast are you going?" he would ask from his car seat in the back.

"Forty," I would answer.

In the rear view mirror, I would see his little head craning up to look over the seat. "No you're not, you're going fifty," he'd accuse. Grudgingly, I'd slow down.

I thought that his pre-teen years would lead toward a more reckless attitude, but I was wrong. The other day we were driving down Alta Vista Street, on our way to a friend's house. I was following a small truck with lawn care implements in the back.

The truck was doing the speed limit, but it felt slower. I don't know why it always feels slow to follow a landscaping truck. Maybe the lawn mowers in the back make it hard to see that the truck is actually moving forward.

Whipping around the truck, I muttered, "He's just too slow for me."

My back seat driver, as usual, had something to say. "How fast was he going?"

"Forty," I replied.

"Mom," the admonishment came. "The speed limit is forty."

"Yes, but he was doing a slow forty," I explained. "I like to do a fast forty."

"What's a 'fast' forty?"

There was a brief silence in the car while I formulated my answer. "Fifty," I admitted, at last.

Now it was Marcus' turn for silence. Finally, he spoke, "Soooo, fifty is not fifty, it's just forty, but more so?"

"Sure," I said, thinking if I couldn't win the debate with reason, confusion was the next best thing.

Still, I slowed the van down a little, to a *medium* forty. I just hope that the Placentia police force appreciates my son's efforts to keep me within the guidelines—er, I mean, speed limits.

## VALENCIA HIGH SCHOOL—SO IT BEGINS

How do you know, as a parent, whether you're planning your child's future success or just filling their hours with busy work until they get a life?

Marcus is in $8^{th}$ grade at Kraemer Middle School, where he is in the Gifted and Talented Education (GATE) program. Recently, we were invited to attend the Valencia High School Academy night to hear about all of the options for his next four years. Since my husband, Dale, had to coach Marcus' soccer practice, I attended the evening alone and briefed him upon my return.

"Well, I'm freaked out," I told him as I walked into the family room.

Valencia has very fine programs for all of their students, and the most rigorous ones were presented at Academy night. Specifically, we heard about the Val Tech program, Advanced Placement (AP) classes and the International Baccalaureate (IB) program. Jim Bell, the assistant principal, emceed the evening, introducing everyone from the principal, Bill Cline, to teachers from all of the core departments. Everyone had something positive to say about the challenges of their classrooms and the rewards of the various programs.

All I could say was, "Holy moly, what should we do?"

Each program has its pluses. The Val Tech program appeals to students with an interest in technology. This would include Marcus, who currently wants a career in designing video games. Of course, I think most 13-year old boys want a career that revolves around video games.

The IB program is very prestigious and guarantees that a passing student will be granted sophomore status in college. For parents who are still wondering how they'll pay their child's tuition, skipping a year can equate to big savings. My husband, Dale, and I would gladly jump on that bandwagon, but...

Video games aside, Marcus has many interests. He's an athlete, he plays the guitar, and he likes to work with animals. He may pick a different career by the time he's 18.

What if we choose the wrong program? What if Marcus becomes single-minded about his life goals and would have been better off in IB? What if he goes through the IB program, then figures out in his junior year of college that he doesn't want to design video games, he wants to be a marine biologist?

What if Marcus becomes a professional athlete (Dale's secret dream) or a rock star (my own fantasy) and none of this matters?

I look back at my own cross-country trip through life: I began college as an art major. Eight years later, I went to Cal State Fullerton for my Bachelor's degree in Computer Science. Twenty years after that, I left the computer business to write. I'm not unhappy about my meandering. My road hasn't been a straight one, but it's been interesting.

As a parent, though, I'd like my son's road to have less bumps in it. I guess I'll have to wait and see.

## SOMETIMES THE ROAD IS BUMPY

They've been doing road construction at the corner of Kraemer and Yorba Linda Boulevards for at least a week. I don't know why, and perhaps I never will. I'm guessing that somebody somewhere knows what's going on, and that I'm just not high enough on the food chain to be informed.

At first, I thought that a traffic signal needed to be replaced. That was the first day of battling the four-way stop sign at the intersection. The way people maneuver a four-way stop in California always reminds me of the scene in the movie "LA Story", where four cars come up to a stop sign, everybody signals for the other cars to go first, then they all burst forward together and collide in the middle. That's pretty much the way it happens.

The only way I can get through the four-way stop is to creep slowly into the intersection, claiming my right to cross while eyeing the other drivers to make certain that they don't run me over. And if I have to turn left, forget it; no one lets me do that without a fight.

Once the signals were operational, I looked to see if they'd installed cameras, or those new left-turn signals that are just guidelines, but they hadn't.

When I saw that there were still bright orange pylons and heavy machinery around, I figured they had to dig up the pavement for some reason. Maybe they had a plumbing leak. Maybe they needed to replace some cables. Or maybe they'd gotten a tip about where to find Jimmy Hoffa. I still didn't know what they were doing, but I merged into the single lane with all of the rest of the clueless drivers and inched slowly through the mess.

By the third or fourth day, when I saw the grass on the median all torn out and the dirt churned up, I thought, is this all about new landscaping? Are they kidding? By this time, I was taking alternate streets that would pass close enough to the construction to see if it was completed yet.

As I wound my way down Palm Avenue and Bradford Street, I couldn't help but think, wouldn't it be nice to have some kind of sign announcing why we're being so inconvenienced? We've known for six months that Walgreen's Drugstore was coming to our corner. Why can't we have a sign that's less generic than "Road Construction Ahead"?

Maybe, "Coming Soon! Sprinklers That Water the Median Instead of Your Car!" Or how about, "Future Site of Drought Resistant, Native Plants"? Perhaps they should just confess their intentions with a sign that says, "Our Goal is to Make Your Commute as Miserable as Possible for at Least Two Weeks, Just Because."

I don't begrudge the workers for doing their jobs. And I know that making improvements sometimes causes temporary inconvenience. I'd just like to know what to look forward to… and when.

## CSI: Placentia

I've always been a sucker for a good mystery, from Agatha Christie to Dean Koontz. So today's glut of crime shows is heaven for me. Every week I am treated to CSI, NCIS, and a host of other shows in which they analyze bits of this and that and figure out who killed the butler.

Even so, sometimes watching the investigators study the crime scene makes me think about what would happen if we came home and had a dead butler in our Placentia kitchen…

First of all, they'd have to buy a lot more plastic bags to pick up all of the evidence. We have a cat and dog who run from room to room, spreading cheer and pet hair everywhere. They might as well save the baggies and just vacuum my house.

And then there's my darling hubby and son, who are not that concerned about clutter or cleanliness. On a recent episode of CSI, they identified a suspect from blades of grass found in a closet. If they found a clump of grass in our closets, they'd have to carbon-date it to figure out which year it was left there.

I will also confess to random acts of grime, having occasionally walked through the house in my riding boots. The investigators might come to the conclusion that the butler was killed in a stall, then dragged into our kitchen.

Fingerprints won't be of any use in our home, either. I try to clean, but my 13-year old son and his friends all feel the need to grip doorways, slap at ceilings and touch everything in a room for no apparent reason. The good news is that I dust so infrequently that the CSI team can use less powder and save money.

Come to think of it, murder is one way of getting your house cleaned professionally.

They usually interview the neighbors on these shows, and find out a lot about the victim's habits. I doubt if they'd have the same luck with our neighbors. We all seem to work for a living around here, so we don't spend a lot of time noticing whether the people next door are fighting, leaving at odd hours, or having wild parties. I imagine their interviews would go something like this:

"So what time did Mr. Carline get home last night?"

"I don't know. I had to work until 9."

"Was Mrs. Carline home all day?"

"I don't know. She only comes out to get the paper and the mail."

"When was the last time you saw their son?"

"When he was four."

"When was the last time you saw their butler?"

"They have a butler?"

Come to think of it, by the time the investigators collected all of the evidence, determined which of it was actually relevant, and identified a suspect, the killer could have changed his name and moved to Fiji. The Carline house could just be the place to commit the perfect crime.

I guess it's a good thing we don't have a butler.

## WHEN TRYING TO BE HELPFUL BACKFIRES

Although my column leans toward the details of daily life, like any good Placentian, I try to stay informed about what's happening in my city. For example, I like to read the news about the On Trac brouhaha in an attempt to wrap my mind around all of that money and where it went.

Having worked in the aerospace industry on several large projects, I understand how such a big job can go so wrong. I've witnessed countless meetings where people put up charts and pointed to how much progress their team had made, only to push the work past the deadline (and over the cliff) because they were still designing the last ten percent that actually made the thing operational.

So now that the money is gone, the participants are pointing fingers and the people are outraged, I find myself thinking about why we wanted to raise the train tracks and lower the streets (or is it the other way round?) in the first place: we wanted to prevent deaths that occur when people try to beat the train. In other words, we're trying to protect people from being stupid.

It's a difficult task, certainly not one that Mother Nature ever did for us. Back in the days of early man, I'll bet Neanderthals had lots of conversations about this.

Caveman 1: "Look, Oog think he can outrun saber-toothed tiger."

Caveman 2: "Oog pretty stupid. Dibs on his spear."

Now we've replaced Mother Nature's job of ensuring the survival of the fittest with keeping everybody safe, even from themselves. We think they can't try to outrun the train, nature's new saber-tooth tiger, if they can't drive, walk, bicycle or otherwise cross the tracks.

Over the years, we've taken a lot of stupid acts away from people, but I don't think we've taken away any stupidity. It just leaks out in other ways.

People used to pile a family of twelve in a sedan and careen through the streets willy-nilly, but now we make them use seat belts, meaning they have to take two cars. Does that stop them from crashing? No, because now the drivers of the two cars talk on their cell phones incessantly while they careen. Wearing seat belts may save their lives, but it can't stop the stupidity.

Men used to get on flying deathtraps called motorcycles and let the wind blow through their hair; now they have to wear helmets to protect their brains if they crash. Of course, I still see motorcyclists on summer days roaring down the street in shorts and flip flops. Clearly, their helmet is protecting a brain that is not often used.

Once I saw a video of a police officer trying to ticket a woman who had carefully driven her car in between the railroad crossing gates that had been lowered for an oncoming train. The woman argued, sincerely and articulately, that it wasn't a crime because her car fit through the space. I'm not saying that she was from the shallow end of the gene pool, but she was definitely in the section with no lifeguard on duty.

I hope that the effort begun by On Trac gets back on track, although I'm a little worried about what people will try when we've stopped them from dashing in front of trains. I'm not trying to say that we shouldn't have these laws, or that the trains shouldn't be separated from cars. They're all good ideas.

I'm just saying that, as the comedian Ron White points out, you can't fix stupid. You can only relieve some of the symptoms.

## LIVING WILD IN THE CITY

"It smells like something's on fire."

These are never good words to hear when you are driving a 10-year old minivan with 150,000 miles on it. Nevertheless, they are exactly what my son, Marcus, said as we drove down Alta Vista Street late last week.

The worst part was that he was right, or at least I thought he was right. My sinuses were so clogged that I only had one working nostril, so I could just smell a glimpse of what was either meat on a grill or hair burning. It didn't matter, since neither of them belonged in my car.

I kept driving while we opened and closed windows, turned various vents on and off, and felt around the dashboard, looking for signs that we should pull over and abandon ship. The smell wasn't getting any stronger, but it wasn't going away.

Suddenly, in the midst of our quest for fire, I saw a shadow trot across the street in front of us. Slowing down, I watched the shape reveal itself in the light before disappearing onto the golf course.

"A coyote!" I exclaimed and looked at Marcus, expecting his mouth to be hanging open like mine.

It wasn't. Smiling, he said, "Yeah."

"I've never seen a coyote in our neighborhood," I said. "On Alta Vista Street! Did you see it?"

"Yeah," he repeated.

As I prattled on and on about how big it was and brazen and I didn't think Placentia was 'wild' enough to have coyotes, it dawned on me that Marcus wasn't sharing my shock and awe.

I asked him, "Aren't you surprised to see a coyote here?"

He gave me that look that his dad gives me sometimes—it's a bemused smirk that Dale uses when he thinks I am rambling on about nothing.

"Not really," he told me.

I gave him my stare of sarcasm, wishing I had a daughter to inherit my raised eyebrows.

"Oh, you see a lot of coyotes around here? Doing what? Having lattes down at Starbucks?"

"I'm just saying that it's not completely surprising, since we have coyotes in southern California."

Why did I have to be the mother of a reasonable son?

This led to a conversation about what kind of animal would he be surprised to see on Alta Vista. A mastodon, for example, would be a surprise for a lot of reasons. In contrast, we have so many opossums wandering across our block wall that the only way for them to surprise us is if they start driving golf carts. A deer would definitely be a novelty, but raccoons would not. Recently, I watched one of the neighbor cats chase a young raccoon out of its yard.

"What about a mouse?" I wondered.

"Mom, if I could actually see a mouse run across the road at 10 o'clock at night, I'd be amazed that my eyesight was that good," he told me.

By the time we got home, I ran in to tell Dale about the coyote, expecting him to be at least mildly excited about it. Let's just say that his reaction was further proof that Marcus is his son.

It wasn't until the next morning that I remembered our original discussion about the burning smell. I decided that the car must not have been on fire. If it had been, I'm sure the coyote would have noticed.

## KEEPING ABREAST OF THE NEWS

A few weeks ago, a friend of mine emailed me.

"What is going on with the Placentia police chief?" she asked. "I heard he was on suspension." She was, of course, referring to John Schaefer, who has subsequently retired.

I told her all I had heard was that he'd been put on administrative leave. What I didn't tell her was that I had to do a quick search through the newspaper and the Internet to come up with even that much information.

To keep up on current events, I read two newspapers, and four news websites every day, so I really should have known more.

But the truth is, I don't really read the "real" news.

I know I should be interested in international news, the war in Iraq, and events in our community. But every time I try to read a serious article, I get distracted by news of the weird.

Today, for example, I had every intention of reading about the talks being held in the Middle East, and how Condoleeza Rice got everyone to the table. Unfortunately, there was an article on the same page about a mystery nun who is at the center of getting Pope John Paul II beatified. It's so full of interesting quirks that I couldn't resist, beginning with the idea of a "mystery nun."

It's always been like this for me. Odd pieces of trivia get stuck in my brain while important information is released back into the wild. As a student, I spent hours in my World History class studying how Charlemagne rose to power. As soon as I took the test, all of the names and dates scampered from my memory, never to return.

On the other hand, our teacher once mentioned about learning to ride an elephant, and why you always want to ride behind the ears. That casual tidbit remains implanted in my mind, easily available for party conversations.

So you can see why, instead of finding out why those eight federal prosecutors got fired by the Justice Department, I want to know about the toad the size of a small dog that was discovered in Darwin, Australia. First of all, I can't think of a more appropriate place to find an oddity than Darwin, Australia. Second, it made me wonder, if you touch a toad the size of a dog, will it give you warts the size of a cat?

And, while it would be nice to know more about the Metrolink station planned for Placentia, it's not as fascinating as the retriever who performed the Heimlich maneuver on his owner. I can't imagine our Corgi dog rising up to that challenge. Now, if there was a life-saving maneuver that involved running into your shins at full speed, he could do that.

I think that I could read a lot more of the hard-hitting news if it had more of a quirky edge to it. What if the article I tried to read today about Bush and Putin discussing the missile defense plan over the phone, mentioned whether they had to pay for peak hours? It quoted a long-time analyst as saying that the relationship between our two countries is in serious trouble. What if the article suggested that they see a counselor? Maybe there's a Nuke-Anon in their area.

Some people complain that too much entertainment has already seeped into mainstream news. I can't disagree. No one wants to read in-depth articles. They want the short, spicy version.

But for me, I need that little dose of the odd with the normal. It helps me remember what made the news, well, newsworthy.

## POMP AND CIRCUMSTANCE, CIRCUMSTANCE AND POMP

I recently read a news item about students in Illinois who didn't receive their diplomas because their families cheered as they crossed the stage. While I think it's unfair to punish the children for their families' actions, I understand the school's reasons for trying to keep the noise down.

After all, we live close enough to Bradford Stadium to hear all of the graduation ceremonies. For four nights in June, we hear "Pomp and Circumstance," along with the announcement of names, although they are somewhat garbled by the time the sound reaches our home.

We also hear air horns.

I first heard that delightful sound when Marcus graduated from Kraemer Middle School. Sitting in the stands at high noon, I was trying not to burst into flames before the last student received their diploma. Suddenly a name was announced and my eardrums were jolted forcibly into my brain from an obnoxious blast of noise. At first, I thought we were having an air raid, but I soon realized that there were more parents in the audience with these little horns from hell. As they pressed their buttons, they also pressed mine.

A year later, I don't remember the names of the students who were honked at. But I still recall the look of horror on their faces as they walked up to get their diplomas.

When I was a child (sometime during the Jurassic era), I performed in many school and church programs. There was always one kid who would mortify his parents by waving and yelling, "Hi, Mom!" at the top of his lungs.

Now it's the kids who are embarrassed.

I've been to concerts, programs, and ceremonies at all of Marcus' schools, and I'm constantly in awe of the parents who behave like they're at a rock concert.

Names are called out, along with general screaming and whooping. Some people even treat segments of the program that don't feature their child as though it's the perfect time to make that call on the cell phone—from their seat, of course.

In movies and TV shows, school programs are formal affairs, where everyone sits and watches in enrapt silence. For some reason, I keep expecting the real world to operate that way, so I spend the first part of the my son's events reminding myself that it doesn't and that I can't control the rest of the audience.

Just as you can't yell "Fire" in a crowded theater, you also can't yell "Shut up" to a room full of enthusiastic parents.

I don't mind hearing "Pomp and Circumstance," every night for a week. Knowing that young people are graduating fills me with hope for the future, and I'm looking forward to sitting in the stands and watching Marcus in his cap and gown. I just don't want to hear the honking.

I've got three years to figure out how to get through the ceremony with my hearing intact. So far, I've thought of a few ideas. I could start a rumor that air horns cause cancer. Or I could recommend that graduation seating be partitioned into Air Horn and Non-Air Horn sections. I've even thought about trying to get air horns banned at graduation ceremonies.

No, that would be too obvious.

# SUMMER SCHOOL AT EL DORADO

By the time this hits the paper, I will be blissfully free of school until September. Marcus' school, that is.

It took every ounce of strength to push my son through the end of the normal school year at Valencia High School. What had begun as an enthusiastic freshman semester had degraded into a foot dragging slog through the last quarter. He finally did manage to raise his grades high enough to earn his tickets to the Weird Al concert, but it was a photo finish.

We breathed a collective sigh of relief for four days, when Marcus started summer school. It seems that no student worth their salt takes the Health and Career Planning courses during the school year. They all take them in the summer, in order to give them three more weeks to whine about getting up early and extort lunch money from their parents.

The worst part about summer school has been driving Marcus to and from El Dorado High School. I have nothing against EDHS, but it would be so much easier to have summer school at Valencia, where Marcus could walk to and from class.

I have some observations about driving my son to school, and dealing with all of the parents who are late to work in the morning, and jockeying for position in the parking lot in the afternoon.

First of all, I noticed that no one has a sense of humor at 7:30 in the morning. Scowling parents shove their cars in spaces that don't exist so that they can push their obstinate teenagers out the door. For those of us who are unfamiliar with the El Dorado campus, we began our week by driving in the exit, going the wrong way, and trying to find a graceful way to correct our mistake. This added to the morning confusion.

It did not add, however, to the other parents' dispositions.

Second, I'm envious of the EDHS parking lot. Compared to Valencia, it's huge. Of course, the size doesn't help at the end of the day, when cars full of teenagers are racing toward the exits, cutting in front of each other, and generally making me want to tattle on all of them—not to their parents, but to their insurance agents.

Which brings me to my third observation: when you get to school early to pick up your child, you see a lot of oddities in the parking lot.

One day, I watched the security personnel try to either escort a young lady back onto campus, or off of it. At one point, a police car got involved while the officer tried to resolve the problem. I don't know whether she ever got back to class or to her home, but I did hear one security guard tell another, "That girl's got attitude to spare."

And then there was the day I watched a driver in a small, silver car driving around the large parking lot. She was making a figure eight across the width of the lot, and all of the marked stalls. The odd part about this is that she drove the same pattern for twenty minutes. Yes, I timed it, because after the first five minutes, I started wondering why anyone would do this for five minutes. After ten minutes, I was enrapt; at twenty minutes, I was dumbfounded.

VHS's parking lot would never allow that kind of antics. It's not wide enough.

Of course, I wouldn't be waiting in Valencia's parking lot, because Marcus would be walking home after school. I can only hope that there'll be summer school at VHS next year, when he's taking Health.

Otherwise, I guess I'll be waiting at El Dorado, watching what happens next.

## MAKING FRIENDS WITH THE NEIGHBORS

I returned to my hometown recently and was reminded of one of the major differences between Decatur, Illinois, and Placentia.

And I don't mean the palm trees, mild climate or lack of soybean processing factories. I'm talking about isolation.

When I told friends that it took me three hours to drive from Chicago Midway Airport to Decatur, they pictured a drive like the one from here to Santa Barbara, on freeways through mostly populated areas.

It's not like that in Illinois. When the sidewalk ends in Decatur, there's nothing but farmland until the next city, flat farmland full of corn, soybeans, and livestock. The only population between Decatur and the next town are the cows.

By contrast, Placentia is nestled in among other cities, tucked in so snugly that you can't tell where it ends and the next town begins. Consequently, what I think of as "my neighborhood" may encompass two or three cities.

For example, I typically do my grocery shopping at Albertson's. Until a month ago, I thought the store was in Placentia. It is on Placentia Avenue, after all.

As it turns out, it's in Fullerton.

So is the Ralph's on Yorba Linda Boulevard, although the Office Max, across from the Ralph's is in Placentia. Apparently, Bradford is the boundary to the west.

Or is it?

Kraemer Park is to the west of Bradford, and it's in Placentia, as are most of the homes in that area.

Oh, I know how it is with these cities. Due to their growth and the towns around them, their boundary lines are all squiggled. They didn't mean for the houses on one side of a street to be in a different city than the other side. The founding families probably envisioned lovely, rectangular towns with nice, square borderlines.

I'm sure that everyone started with a nice location to plant a flag and claim in their father's name. Then another family came along and wanted to share the burden of retrieving water from the well, so they joined forces.

Time passed, and more families wanted to band together and split the cost of sidewalks and streetlights. Pretty soon, a city was born.

I wish I could have been here to see the last parcels of land being divvied up between Brea, Fullerton, and Placentia. It must have been an intense negotiation.

Brea: "We want Imperial and Kraemer."

Fullerton: "Why should you get it?"

Brea: "Because you already have two Mervyn's and two Targets."

Placentia: "Can we at least have Bradford and Yorba Linda Boulevard?"

Fullerton: "Why?"

Placentia: "So we can have our own Starbuck's."

Brea and Fullerton: "No!"

Okay, I'm fairly certain that no one knew what stores would be where, so I may be exaggerating.

At least the three cities can share Tri-City Park without fighting over it. If our Tri-City Park Authority can get along, anyone can. In fact, their ability to play nicely together could be used as a model to resolve problems in the Middle East.

So I suppose that my little Placentia neighborhood is really my little Tri-City neighborhood, even if it is all in a two-mile radius of my house. And I wouldn't trade it for all of the cornfields in Illinois.

Although, sometimes I have to break out my passport to visit Irvine.

## CAR WASHING AND PEOPLE WATCHING

A reader complained recently that I am self-absorbed, never get out in my community and "belong in the land of gracious living." We'll leave the dig at our neighboring city alone, because I am certain that it is filled with lovely people who do all kinds of good deeds.

But since this column is about how I spend my days in Placentia, I'll focus on my own faults.

First of all, I'd love to be self-absorbed, but I don't have the time. I'm a little busy, driving my son everywhere, running errands, and teaching children about horses. Last week, I realized I've been so busy that I haven't even had the time to wash my ten-year old minivan.

For a year.

Frankly, I'm so used to the dog hair, stall shavings and Albertson's receipts floating around my car, I could have gone another year without washing it. However, I needed to take a group of people to the Weird Al Yankovic concert, and I thought they might object to sitting in so much dirt. So I went to the car wash for some extreme cleaning.

I like the local car wash. The staff is friendly, and it's better for the environment than washing my car in my driveway, although I think the name, Car Wash of America, makes it sound like I should see license plates from every state.

When I drove up, the same man greeted me as the last time I was there. He acted happy to see me, even though I just brought him the filthiest car on the planet.

"Do you have an hour to wait for our Five Star Service?" he asked.

"No, I have to get to a concert."

He was still smiling, but I could see disappointment in his eyes.

"Next time, I promise," I said.

After paying, I walked down the hallway to the patio, past all of the people who were following their car through the viewing window, making certain that they got the soap and wax they paid for. Actually, I'm guessing—I don't know why people watch their cars go through the wash.

On the patio, there were two types of people sitting and waiting. One group watched for the attendant to raise his hand, then leaped up to claim their vehicle. The other group ignored the attendant until he had honked their horn repeatedly, after which they casually wandered over to their cars.

I was in the first group, although I tried to look like I was in the second.

The workers all bustled around from one car to the next, speaking to each other occasionally. I don't speak Spanish, but it appeared that they were all business, pointing to rags and bottles while they talked.

Even though I said I didn't have an hour to get my car washed, it took almost that long to get the first layer of grime off. I watched the attendant open doors and climb in and out of the seats while other vehicles came and went, and I began to wonder whether he had a quota to meet.

Reaching into my purse, I took out a bigger tip.

Finally, he held up his hand, and I scampered over to claim my minivan. This was one of those moments I wished I could speak better Spanish so I could lavish him with compliments, instead of smiling and telling him "thank you" while I handed him money. He had worked so hard, I wanted to reward him with more.

My irate reader wants me to get out in my community and talk about interesting people. I think that the people I run into on a daily basis are all interesting, whether they are washing cars, checking groceries, or repairing my home.

And they're all in my community.

## FUNDRAISING TO SUPPORT OUR SCHOOLS

By the time anyone reads this column, school will have started, and there will be a collective sigh throughout the Placentia-Yorba Linda School District. As much as we adore our children, most of us are happy to ship them off to their teachers in September, if only to keep from hearing "I'm bored" one more time.

We think that, once we've filled out the dozen forms in duplicate and paid all of the fees, we can sit back and watch our children learn. As parents, we are lulled into a sense of completion.

We are wrong.

Lurking around the corner, waiting to pounce, are the fundraisers, events designed to wring every last moment from our busy days so that our children can have uniforms, trips, and a banquet at the end of the year.

Elementary school eased us into this yearly habit. The PTA sent out one catalogue of wrapping paper and knick-knacks for us to sell to friends and family. I was still working at Raytheon, and could sell to my work associates. Dale worked the other side of the company, and his family.

Kraemer Middle School continued the tradition of one organization, one fundraiser. I was no longer working at Raytheon, but my horse trainers bought a few things, and Dale still had Raytheon.

And then Marcus graduated to Valencia High School and the stakes were higher. In high school, students are encouraged to be in a lot of activities. And, with every activity, there's a need for something that, apparently, money can't buy. Sure, we could just write a check, but our kids still bring home the catalogues, complete with a sales goal and the admonishment from teachers and coaches to "sell, sell, sell!"

We started off last year with choir, selling cookie dough. Marcus sold his heart out to family, friends and neighbors, and I helped separate the orders when they came in.

Then soccer season came and we sold cookie dough again. Most of our family and friends already had their yearly dough and didn't need more. Marcus had such a poor response from the neighbors that he didn't even try them again. But he managed to sell a few boxes.

Over the summer, Marcus joined the cross country team. To raise funds, they sold—yes, cookie dough. We now have 14 boxes of frozen cookies in our two freezers, and I'm actually afraid of this year's fundraisers.

Our choir is attempting a fundraiser that will, hopefully, bring in a lot of money. We're raffling off a new car. I recently attended a booster meeting to discuss raising funds, and we talked about the cost of the tickets, the process for keeping the raffle above-board, and how to advertise effectively.

At $30 a ticket, the price seemed high to some members, until someone pointed out that Villa Park raffled off a Mercedes last year for $100 a ticket. We're only raffling off either a Ford Mustang or Edge, so the price is probably right.

I plan to buy a ticket, even though I don't believe I'll win. I'm not a particularly lucky woman, but the chance to buy a $25,000 car for $30 is irresistible.

Of course, the price of the tickets and the prize to be won means that the tickets must all be accounted for and the entries monitored closely. And, at the conclusion, an independent accountant will verify that everything was done correctly. So the ticket sales must cover the cost of the accountant, plus the costs of advertising. The booster club is hoping that a lot of people will be thinking like me and want to get a new car for $30.

And I'm hoping that it's a successful fundraiser, because I just can't buy any more cookie dough.

## A VALENTINE ROMANCE IN PLACENTIA

Suggestions, I get suggestions…

Friends, family and readers occasionally give me ideas for my column. Sometimes I use them, and sometimes I smile wanly and write about the laundry instead.

I received an interesting suggestion this week from a company who saw my name on an Internet list of columnists. "Dear Gayle," it said, "Perhaps you are looking for a cute Valentine's Day column idea."

This company writes personalized romance novels, using you and your significant other as heroes in the setting of your choice. They offer "mild" or "wild" versions, depending upon how spicy you like your virtual love life, and invent romantic adventures on tropical islands, at dude ranches, or any place in between.

When I explained to their representative that my column revolves around my hometown of Placentia, they countered that one of their new plots is a water-based story set in Huntington Beach. They thought it would be appropriate for my audience because we're in Orange County, too.

I didn't have the heart to tell them that Huntington Beach and Placentia are in Orange County the way that Hawaii and New York are in the United States – on opposite ends of the boundary lines and impossible to drive from one to the other.

But I did think about proposing Placentia as a new setting for their novels. From the paths of Tri-City Park to the cozy tables at Sophia's, our city could be a romantic getaway for two.

I even experimented with a few scenes, using Dale and me as the fantasy couple. Here's an example of a Valentine's Day escapade at Tri-City Park:

*They strolled leisurely, through the grass, arms around each other, Gayle's head resting on his shoulder. Pausing beneath the spreading tree, Dale cupped her face in his hands. The realization of how much he loved her hit him like a soccer ball in the head.*

*"Little help, Mister," yelled the boy as he ran past.*

*"Maybe we shouldn't stand so close to the Tuffree soccer fields," she suggested.*

*Walking over to the lake, they watched the sun's rays ripple across the water. Dale found a shady spot in the grass and started to sit down.*

*"Oh, not there," Gayle warned. "There's duck poop on the grass."*

*Looking around the area, he finally led her to a park bench and pulled her down to his lap.*

*"Oof," he exhaled.*

*"I'm sorry," she said. "I guess I shouldn't have eaten that extra taco."*

*Sliding next to him, they sat, entwined, whispering words of love and desire.*

*"Did you get more orange juice at the store?" he asked.*

*"I thought we could pick some up on our way home. The dog's out of food, too."*

*As they began to kiss, Gayle became aware of a constant thudding on her leg. Pulling back from Dale, she asked, "Are you kicking me in the shin?"*

*"No," he said, a little irritated.*

*Looking down, they saw that a goose had wandered over from the lake and was pecking her.*

*"Maybe it's time to leave," she said. "We have to be home in time for the Valencia Choir to come over and sing for you."*

*"Why would the choir sing to me?"*

*"It's their singing telegram fundraiser for Valentine's Day. I ordered you a song."*

*Rolling his eyes, Dale told her, "Then we better get going."*

Okay, it's not champagne and caviar, but this is why I don't write romances—reality always intrudes.

Their Huntington Beach novel is called The Shore Thing. Maybe the Placentia version could be The Real Thing.

## SWINGIN' WITH THE PARKS AND REC DEPARTMENT

Throughout our marriage, Dale and I have tried to have "date night." They say it's a great way for couples to rise above the daily responsibilities of home and family, and rekindle the romance. It sounds like a good idea, although I don't know how a couple avoids those topics, even at a fancy restaurant.

Dale and I have had limited success with this. When Marcus was little, we had to find a babysitter. Now that he's older, we have to coordinate our schedules.

So, when I received the Placentia Quarterly last December, I decided to sign us up for a class. I thought it would be a great way to get us out of the house together and focused on something besides Marcus' soccer schedule.

What I really wanted was a cooking class, but there weren't any of those. We had Wednesdays at eight available, and the only class at that time was West Coast Swing. Dale likes to dance, and is a good sport about learning new steps. In addition, we're going on a cruise to Alaska in June; I've seen the brochures, and we can go out dancing every night if we want. This was going to be fun.

The only thing that could go wrong was—me.

I used to be in a dance group, Swing Shift. We performed American dances from the 20's through the 40's at various events, from the Orange County Fair, to the opening of the 105 Freeway. One of the dances we did is called the Lindy Hop. It is a precursor to most swing dancing, fast paced and fun.

It is also kind of like West Coast Swing, and kind of different. They are both partnered dances where the man draws the woman toward him, then sends her away. In West Coast, the movements are in six-count steps. In Lindy, they are eight-counts. The Lindy Hop is bouncy, with knees bent and hips swiveling. West Coast is danced very upright and smooth.

We met several other couples in our first class, and had fun learning the steps. Although I missed the extra two counts of the Lindy, I managed to maintain the six-count required by West Coast.

"Step, step, triple step, triple step," the instructor kept repeating.

And then she started the music. Instead of "step, step," my knees went "bounce, bounce," and my hips swiveled back and forth. My upright West Coast style left the building, pushed aside by the jumpin', jivin' Lindy.

"Try walking, heel-toe," the instructor suggested as she observed us. "You don't want to be on the balls of your feet for the step in."

I smiled and nodded. Step, step, I walked toward Dale, trying to keep my body from swaying to the music.

"You're getting ahead of the count," he growled at me.

It's true, I was. The music was a little slow, so I was dancing the half-counts. I reduced the speed of my triple steps. My step, step became swivel, swivel again.

"Stop that," Dale said.

Before the class was over, I received a lot more suggestions from the instructor, about draping my arms, stepping too far back on count four, anchoring underneath myself, and more. I smiled, nodded, and kept trying.

We've had five of the seven classes now, and I've learned to lower the "bounce" factor, although I'm sure that my body still swivels too much to be a respectable West Coast swing dancer. Hopefully, no one will notice once we hit the dance floor on the ship.

I guess you can take the girl out of Lindy, but you can't take the Lindy out of the girl.

## A LITTLE VOLUNTEER WORK AT THE LIBRARY

I've had a busy month. Over spring break, my girlfriend and I snuck off to Las Vegas to see Spamalot. I was only home for a day before I drove down to Del Mar to see my horse compete at a horse show. And then, the following week, I flew to Dayton, Ohio, to the Erma Bombeck Writer's Workshop, where I met Garrison Keillor, did a stand-up comedy routine, and studied the science of being funny.

But the most fun was waiting for me at home: I finally got to volunteer at the library.

I had been trying to do this for months with no luck. Back in December, I contacted Brenda Benner about volunteering. I managed to get to one of their meetings in February, but that was it. Every weekend, I looked at my busy calendar and just sighed.

Once I returned from Ohio, I unpacked, walked through my messy house, whined a little, then emailed Nancy Tollefson and asked, "What can I do?"

As luck would have it, Sunday was the library's book sale day, so she was happy to have the extra help. Of course, I would have to prove myself worthy.

I arrived at the library at 12:45, just as her email had said. Unfortunately, she hadn't told me where to go, so I spent a few minutes at the front door with everyone waiting to get in, then went around to the back and worked my way through the line of people waiting there. I kept asking everyone if they were volunteers and they kept pointing me forward.

Eventually, I was where I needed to be.

It's a good thing I never came to the library book sale before. Paperbacks for a quarter a piece? Hard covers for fifty cents? My house would be stacked, from floor to ceiling, with books.

Even so, I was surprised to see people buying boxes of books, and by boxes, I mean three and four milk crates on wheels. One lady bought nothing but engineering textbooks. They told me she sells them on eBay.

I can't think of anything that becomes obsolete faster than an engineering textbook, but apparently they're hot sellers on the Internet. As I watched her drag her purchases out the door, I thought about the engineers bidding on those books, and their poor spouses, trying to figure out where to store them all.

Another man with two boxes and a sack full of purchases had some interesting titles, including "Venus on Wheels: Two Decades of Dialog on Disability, Biography, and Being a Woman." The man reminded me of Ned Beatty. I couldn't imagine him reading about Venus, on wheels or off.

But that was nothing, compared to the distinguished, white-haired gentleman who bought, among other books, "The Man in the Red Velvet Dress: Inside the World of Cross-Dressing." You don't want to know where my imagination went with that title.

Later, a couple came in with their three lively children. They tried to shop and contain their kids' energies, and were mostly successful at both. The dad finally laid his purchases on the counter, a stack of children's stories and Conan the Barbarian books. A few minutes later, the mother came back with another Conan.

"They're for my mom," she told me. "She loves them."

*Well, sure*, I thought.

The afternoon passed quickly. According to the other volunteers, it was a light crowd, which was good for me, since it gave me an opportunity to learn what to do, and to get to know everyone. I left feeling energized and useful.

I hope I'm not too busy to do it again.

# PLACENTIA NOIR?

Volunteering at the library was so much fun, I couldn't wait to do it again. My previous adventure at the library was a Sunday book sale. I had a great time, so I was looking forward to another phone call telling me they needed help with something.

After a couple of months, I began to worry that I didn't do as good a job as I thought.

Then, one afternoon, between loads of laundry, someone from the library called; could I help with a special event next Tuesday at 6? I immediately said yes, and went back to folding clothes, thinking about my Tuesday schedule.

Uh-oh. I had two riding lessons that day, one at 4:30 and one at 5:30. I called my 5:30 client and rescheduled, then made a mental list of what else I needed to do. I was all set.

On Tuesday, I put on my jeans, hung a nice outfit in the minivan and headed off to the ranch. I also reminded Dale and Marcus that I would not be home for dinner, and they were on their own. Knowing my son, I reminded Marcus several times—and then left him a note.

As luck would always have it, my 4:30 lesson was late, by twenty minutes. I couldn't possibly extend their time, so we rescheduled that, too. The good news was that I didn't have to hurry to the library, and was able to change clothes, fluff my hair and be back in Placentia fifteen minutes early.

I met Mary Strazdas outside the library, where she was helping one of the featured speakers, Denise Hamilton, with her boxes of books for sale. Mary's title is Reference Librarian, but she was so much more on Tuesday night. For the next three hours, she kept the event running smoothly, from the presentation to the snacks. She also kept me running, which I liked.

As for the presentation, the speakers were delightful. Denise Hamilton, a former crime reporter with the Los Angeles Times, is now the author of several mystery novels that feature, of course, a crime reporter who solves each case. With her was Gary Phillips, another mystery writer whose gritty style is showcased in his books, short stories, and graphic novels.

Together, they discussed a recent project that Denise edited, "Los Angeles Noir", a collection of mystery stories by diverse authors, all set in difference sections of L.A. Though the audience was small, Denise and Gary were generous with their time, happily answering questions and talking about what defines "noir."

As they spoke, I couldn't help thinking about writing an "Orange County noir" book—which was hard to do without laughing. Orange County doesn't have a dark, moody reputation. I can't imagine, for example, Humphrey Bogart saying, "Of all the frozen yogurt joints in all the towns in all the world…"

It's possible that Orange County is too well lit to be noir.

After Gary and Denise left, the real work began. Mary and I schlepped water bottles and books, cleaned the coffee pot, and put out the trash. My volunteer work ended at nine, when I headed for home.

I do wish the event had attracted more people. Including Mary and me, there were probably ten people in the audience. Mary wondered if she had not advertised enough in the right places. Gary wondered if it had something to do with the Laker game that was on TV. I'm thinking that maybe Orange County residents couldn't quite connect with an L.A. subject matter. Maybe we could get a better attendance if we discussed murder and mayhem in Placentia.

I hope I'm asked to volunteer for that event.

## A GREAT WAY TO DISCOVER OUR PAST

One of the nice things about volunteering at the Placentia Library is that I learn something new every time. A few months ago, I got to hear authors Denise Hamilton and Gary Phillips talk about what defines Los Angeles 'noir' stories, and how they write them. As a writer, their process fascinated me. As a volunteer, the chance to help my library made me feel like a better person.

Last Monday, I got another chance to add a few points to my Karmic index. I got the call to come and help at an evening program. I didn't know what kind of presentation was scheduled, so I checked the Placentia Library website and found that someone was going to be talking about genealogy.

I arrived at 6:15 that evening to help Mary Strazdas set up the food and drink. Since the weather had been so hot and the meeting room tends to be warm with a lot of bodies in it, Mary decided to serve cold bottles of water instead of coffee. She showed me where to get the ice to fill the coolers and I began icing down the bottles.

As I leaned over the second chest to pour in the ice cubes, my earring popped out of my ear and fell between the bottles and the ice. It sank to the bottom, completely irretrievable, unless I wanted to start dragging bottles out. I wondered if the earring would stick to a bottle and be extracted by an unsuspecting library patron. I was glad it wasn't Halloween, when I usually wear my scary pumpkin jewelry.

In the end, I did the next best thing to digging around in the chest: I took off my other earring and tried to remember to find the lost one when the meeting ended.

The talk about genealogy was very interesting. Norma Keating gave a lot of information, mostly about how to document what you find out about your family tree, and a little about where to find your tree's various branches. She listed many websites and research centers where people could dig for their roots.

It sounded like a full-time job, one that could keep paper mills in business for years. According to Norma, for every piece of information you find, you need to keep a record of when and where you obtained this data. I don't really know why, but the rest of the audience did, and were happy about the sample log sheets she provided. Unlike me, the rest of the audience were already hot on their own family trails.

I have mixed feelings about digging around in my own tree. A few of my relatives did enough study to find that part of the family came from Hesse, Germany. My parents thought these relatives were silly for wanting this information. From the few stories they told me, I think they knew enough to not want to know more.

"I don't know if I'd have the time to do this," I told Mary.

"You might find all of the skeletons in your closet," she said.

I thought about this. My great-grandfather started a riot and burned down my dad's high school. He was 98 years old when he did this. My aunt killed her husband with a butcher knife, and I have cousins who used to stage car accidents in order to collect the insurance. My family covered all of the deadly sins, and I could name names.

After the presentation, I put the leftover food away and emptied the ice chests. There, at the bottom, was my missing earring. I decided that finding my long-lost relatives may be interesting, but finding lost jewelry is more useful.

## FUN AND FUNDRAISING WITH AUTHORS

I like to help the Placentia Library, and I like to eat, so it made perfect sense to attend the Placentia Library Friends Foundation's Author's Luncheon, which was held at the Alta Vista Country Club. It was the first time I went to their yearly event, and the second time I've been to the country club.

Although I was very excited to meet the authors, and have lunch with some of the people I've met by volunteering, I confess I had a couple of purely selfish motives. First, my own first novel, Freezer Burn, will be released in a couple of weeks, so I'm always interested in how other authors market their books. Second, I've already started writing the next book in the series, and, since my books are set in Placentia, I needed to scope out the country club for one of the scenes.

The country club is very pretty. We were in one of the large meeting rooms, with floor-to-ceiling windows overlooking the golf course. Not being a golfer, I'm not certain if we were viewing a green or a tee; men in shorts and polo shirts kept wandering around, scratching their heads. Maybe this course has a "thinker's green."

Lunch was very nice. I sat with Nancy Tollefson, a member of the Placentia Library Friends Foundation, and several others. Nancy spent part of her time visiting and part of it keeping the luncheon schedule moving. Each table was graced with one of the library's "celebrity waiters" who helped to serve drinks, clear away plates, and more.

The event was as fun as it was informative. City Administrator Troy Butzlaff served the laughs as he emceed, dressed in a Roman toga with a laurel wreath adorning his head. He introduced "Super Librarian", library director Jeanette Contreras in a clever Superman-style costume, complete with cape. Super Librarian announced, with a wink, that Jeanette couldn't make the festivities, so she was helping out by presenting all of the people who had helped make the luncheon possible.

It was a large group, and I couldn't help but feel envious, having put together the Valencia Choir's Dinner Theater back in February with about a tenth of the staff. Maybe I should call on some of these folks for next year's dinner.

The three authors were very interesting. Jo Ann De Matteo wrote a historical romance, Cranberry Lake, and Ann Mauer wrote The Magic Eye, which is historical fiction. They told some fascinating stories of how they got interested in their subject matter, as well as how they wrote their books.

The third author, Jeri Westerson, wrote a murder mystery, which of course, attracted my attention. Her story is set in the Middle Ages, and she told a hysterical anecdote about hanging a large chunk of meat on her children's swing-set to practice stabbing it with a dagger, so she could describe it in her book properly. Ah, the things authors will do for authenticity.

We were also treated to songs from Stephanie Song, the Miss Placentia Teen 1st Runner-up, who coincidentally is a VHS student and has been one of Marcus' classmates since Kraemer Middle School. I happen to know that, not only is Stephanie talented, she is a member of the National Honor Society, which makes her a smart cookie, too. I love to see our neighborhood kids excel, and it made her performance even more enjoyable.

The luncheon proved to be thoroughly successful for me. I met new authors, chatted with old friends, and got more ideas for the next book. Maybe someday I'll even be one of the authors at the Author's Luncheon.

## SHARING BIG NEWS WITH MY LITTLE CITY

Have you ever had one of those big events to plan and execute, the kind that take your attention from the rest of your life? Birthday bashes, anniversary parties, weddings, all suck your focus away from balancing your checkbook, returning phone calls, and sometimes breathing in and out.

My big event happened last week. I threw a party for my debut novel, Freezer Burn. When you get a book published, it's customary to have a launch party. I've seen pictures of these parties, but I've never actually attended a book launch, so I didn't know what to do. Unfortunately, I couldn't find a Launch Party for Dummies book to help me.

It took several months to decide on what I wanted. Actually, since my novel is set in Placentia, I wanted to invite all the city's residents to Capone's Restaurant for dinner and drinks. Dale nixed that idea, so I had to think of something else.

Plan B occurred to me when I talked to my publisher about possible venues; I had just taken a dance class at the Backs Community Building in Kraemer Memorial Park. In my novel, the first body is discovered against that building. Of course, that made it a perfect place to gather friends and neighbors, and celebrate.

By the time Sunday arrived, the hard work had been done and the fun started. My friend Robin and her son, Ryan, helped Marcus and I decorate the Main Room, while Dale stayed at home and worked with Bedazzled caterers on the after-party for our family and friends. All that was left, as the clock ticked down to launch time, was to wonder how many people would show up.

By three o'clock, we had a good crowd, not only of friends and family, but column readers, too. It was so nice to meet people who have sent me emails about my stories. Marjie was there, as well as the very funny Warren and his wife Claudine. I also met Jane, the lady who is originally from my hometown of Decatur, Illinois. Nancy Tollefson from the Placentia Library stopped by, and so did fellow authors DeAnna Cameron, Teresa Burrell, and Joanna Keating-Velasco.

After some schmoozing, I gave a little talk about my book. Although Freezer Burn is a mystery, I explained there is no graphic violence, or sex. It's about Peri Minneopa, a former housekeeper who is now a private investigator. She goes to a client's home to help him clean his freezer and finds a severed hand inside. As they say, mayhem ensues.

I also told the crowd why I set the story in Placentia. I have a lot of logical reasons, but basically, I've lived in this town for 25 years, and I like it. It's got a small town feeling, even in the middle of southern California sprawl.

After the talk, I signed books, laughed with everyone, and awarded some prizes. I gave some books away to people who answered questions correctly, and I raffled off a basket of goodies, and gave the proceeds to the Valencia High School Choir. Everyone left with a smile on their face, including me.

I don't know if it was a perfect book launch party, but it went the way I planned, so I'm calling it a success. Like those other big events, it was as difficult as planning a wedding, or maybe even more so, since the bride doesn't provide the entertainment. That's usually the drunken cousin's job.

But now the real work starts: selling more books. I should be able to do that and keep breathing, right?

# IN PLACENTIA, WE LOVE TO READ

Last weekend, I got the chance to gather with my fellow Placentians, and have a good time. We were at the Placentia Library for their Summer Reading Celebration. Library director Jeanette Contreras and her staff put together a cornucopia of events, from crafts and rides, to storytelling and movies.

And the most fun part was that it was all free—even the food! I'm talking about pasta lunches with salad and rolls, hot dogs, pizza, and more.

Theoretically, I was there to promote my book, but in reality I just wanted to meet and talk to people, as well as show support for our library. I admit, I was a little worried in the morning; the event was scheduled to begin at 11 a.m. but by 10:45, the Civic Center still had more workers than attendees. Fifteen minutes later, however, people just started showing up, and kept trickling in for the next three hours.

My booth faced Chapman Avenue. I had my books displayed, along with a basket of goodies to be raffled off, and my “decorations”—two gnomes, a picket fence, and a life-sized cardboard replica of Dean Martin. Since my book is titled “Freezer Burn”, Jeanette sat me next to the Sno-Cone booth, and gave me a cooler filled with freezer pops to give to everyone. She also gave me a student volunteer, Manuel.

Manuel was a delightful young man, very bright, and a voracious reader. Since we were spending the next few hours together, I chatted with him, about the things adults like to discuss with teenagers. I’m pretty sure this annoys them, but it amuses us old folks.

I found out that he is a student at El Dorado High School, although his brother attended Valencia. He was volunteering at the library to fulfill his forty hours of community service, required for graduation from high school here in the Placentia-Yorba Linda Unified School District.

“How many hours have you completed already?” I asked him.

“None.”

“Oh. What grade are you in?”

He smiled a little. “I’m a senior this year.”

I couldn’t resist. “Didn’t your mother remind you about getting this done earlier?”

“Yeah, but she nags me so much, I kind of tune her out.”

I made a mental note to go home and thank Marcus for listening to me about the important things, and to lighten up on the nagging, at least about the small stuff.

While Manuel handed out freezer pops, I talked to the people who came by… and talked and talked. I met people who read my column, and stopped by to say hello. I saw a couple of people I used to work with at Raytheon, one of whom was working the event and one who heard about the celebration and came by to see me. I even met a famous horror writer who lives in Fullerton, and was incredibly gracious for a man who writes about wicked monsters that eat people.

At the end of the day, it felt like I should have paid money for the experience. I raised a little cash for the library, sold a few books, but more importantly, had a grand time with the people of Placentia. One of the volunteers and I were sharing our memories of the day, and I mentioned how much I enjoy living here.

"I haven't lived here that long," she said, "But I really like this city. It's so homey."

She's exactly right. Placentia isn't just the city where my house is parked, it's home.

## WHEN YOUR NEW TOWN BECOMES YOUR HOME TOWN

I have to travel to the Midwest this week to attend a mystery writer's convention, after which I'll skip over to my birthplace to speak at two library events. Decatur, Illinois is where I was born and raised, but I hesitate to call it my hometown.

I give that title to Placentia.

I've lived in Placentia longer than I lived in Decatur, which I think makes that statement true, technically. Placentia is my hometown, because it's the town where I've made my home.

The thing is, I consider myself an accidental resident. When I graduated from Cal State Fullerton in 1983 and began making more money as a software engineer, I looked around north Orange County for a new house. My lovely realtor, Mary Heim, helped me look in Fullerton, Brea, Yorba Linda, and Placentia.

The nicest house was in Placentia. It was the right layout, at the right price, in the right location.

A few years later, I needed to move. Again, Mary and I went schlepping through the county, only to arrive back at Placentia. I lived quite happily at Placentia Lakes, married Dale, had Marcus, and suddenly needed a bigger place.

Guess where we found the next house? Of course, this time we were looking for good schools as well as a good neighborhood. Now that Marcus is a senior, I think the Placentia-Yorba Linda educational system has served him well.

Last weekend, I thought a lot about my continual choice of this town, as I participated in the Placentia Heritage Festival. No matter what I've been offered for the past 25 years, I've always chosen Placentia.

Is it all about the real estate?

Maybe it's about the rolling green boulevards on Chapman and Alta Vista Streets. Maybe it's that courtyard where you can check a book out of the library, then stop in at City Hall to schedule a birthday party at one of the parks, and finally pop into the Police Department to say hello.

Or maybe there's something about a little town, squished into the middle of a lot of other towns, that holds a heritage festival every year, complete with a parade, to celebrate its residents, its schools, and its businesses.

The Heritage Festival was, quite frankly, a blast. I was supposed to promote and sell my book, but I was having so much fun talking to people, I had to remind myself why I was there. I saw friends I used to work with, and parents I used to see at soccer games. I also met column readers and shared a laugh over how much their lives mirrored my own. Even Councilman Scott Nelson stopped by to chat, which was nice.

When I did remember to sell my books, I'd offer free bookmarks, saying, "This is for my debut novel, a murder mystery set in Placentia."

Usually, they were interested enough to stop and hear the plot, but one of the police officers walking past told me, "There are no murders in Placentia."

"That's why it's a mystery," I replied.

He still didn't buy a book, but I managed to sell enough to make my publisher happy, and I had a good time doing it, so the day was a success.

Tomorrow I get on a plane to tell the readers in Decatur why I chose Placentia as the setting for my mystery. I plan to give them a lot of logical reasons about a place that has a homey feel, yet is part of a larger population. But I know the top reason.

It's my hometown.

## A LITTLE LIBRARY LOVE

This Friday, I get the privilege of being the guest speaker at the Placentia Library Friends Foundation Annual Meeting. Everyone is invited, and I hope a lot of people attend. Supporting our library is important—plus, I hear there will be cookies.

I still remember my first trip to the library. I was six years old and had just learned to print my name, so my dad took me to the Decatur Public Library for a library card. Our library was a huge, ornate building with stone steps that seemed a mile wide for my little legs.

It was an exciting moment, to stand in front of the librarian and fill out the card. You had to fill it out while she watched, I guess, so your parents wouldn't sneak around and do it for you.

Unfortunately, in the excitement, my penmanship got a little out of control and I printed outside the box. Since this was several (hundred) years ago, I don't remember the librarian's exact words, but they went something like this:

"Tsk, tsk, we didn't keep our letters in the box, did we? I'm afraid we can't give you a library card if you can't sign your name smaller."

She gave me a practice card and showed me and my broken heart the door.

I went home, conquered the box, and then forced my dad to drive me back to the library that day, where I wrote so neatly the librarian swooned and the rest of the library erupted in wild applause. At least, that's what my six-year old self remembers, which is why I should never write a memoir.

My family didn't own a lot of books, so that library was my literary home for years. It was like having infinite worlds at my fingertips. I fell in love with the place as much as the stories it held. The hushed silence and smell of bound paper was as delicious as any sugar-coated treat for me. In time, I even learned the Dewey Decimal system and could navigate my way through all the shelves.

Our relationship cooled when I discovered the Lord of the Rings trilogy. The books were so popular, you could only check them out for a week and there was a waiting list. Even I couldn't read that fast, so I saved every penny from my allowance and bought my own copies. I discovered the luxury of having books on my shelves that I could re-read whenever I wanted.

Now I have a solid wall of books in my house, mostly classics purchased at used bookstores. Lately, I've been accumulating autographed books written by my author friends, and Dale is purchasing books to read for his book club. We're getting rather over-booked. In theory, you can never have too many books, but we now have too many books for our shelves.

Maybe it's time for more shelves.

So I'm going back to my library. I can check books out, enjoy them, and then give them back to the library for someone else to enjoy. If I find I'm checking the same book out to re-read, then I'll consider purchasing it. Otherwise, it's like taking a vacation to a new place. You have a great time, but you probably won't return because there are so many other lands to explore.

I've already got my library card, but I hope Jeanette Contreras, our librarian, is a little more understanding about my signature. I haven't thought inside the box since I was six years old.

## MY FIRST PLACENTIA LOVE LETTER

I've been writing this column for six years, and I'd write it for sixty more if I could live that long. Not only have I gotten to know a lot of people in Placentia, sharing my experiences with readers has given me a more positive attitude over life's little problems.

Who knew plumbing leaks could put a smile on my face?

People kept asking me why I didn't put out a book of my columns. After all, every bookstore has a shelf bulging with Erma Bombeck collections. So I approached several publishers with the idea: I have columns and I have readers. A book of columns would be easy to market.

The publishers were not as convinced.

"It sounds great," they all said. "But you're not famous. Call us when you're Dave Barry."

When I'm Dave Barry, they'll be calling me.

I decided to take advantage of the Amazon program for publishing your own book, in both paperback and digital form. It should have been easy. Throw a bunch of columns together and slap on a title.

Except the engineer in me couldn't do that. I thought about how to organize my book. Should I group them according to subject matter? Some columns were easier to group than others. Perhaps I should just go with the order in which they were published. Should I include all the columns for one year, or pick and choose across years?

Eventually, after months of indecision, I asked myself, what would Erma do?

The answer came immediately. I'd do what I've been doing for six years. Tell a story.

I wrote about how I wrote to the Placentia News-Times to ask if they could use a little humor, and went to their office to discuss the possibility. Then I wrote about the excitement of seeing my words in print every week, all the miscommunications with my boss, and the feedback from the community.

As I wrote my story of becoming a humor columnist, I wove in columns that resonated with my readers and my family.

When the book was complete, I knew exactly what its title should be: What Would Erma Do? Confessions of a First Time Humor Columnist.

The next step was to get some cover art. I know how crucial a good cover is, to catch the reader's eye. For a humor book, I needed something whimsical, in bright colors. Fortunately, Marcus was in choir with a girl whose dad, Joe Felipe, is a graphic designer. I had seen his work on our choir programs, and knew he was good, so I contacted him.

Joe gave me just what I wanted. My cover has vivid swoops of color, with a cartoon version of me, looking very thoughtful. It's a pity I can't actually be the cartoon version of me—she looks a lot younger.

Using Createspace wasn't difficult, but having never published my own book, it took me a couple of rounds to get a finished product. Their digital platform service was much easier, and I got it on Kindle, then discovered a site called Smashwords that formats a book into several electronic formats and offers it for sale.

Now I try to tell everyone about my book without being obnoxious, and check my Amazon rankings more often than I should. My author friends say it takes time to start selling, but it's hard to relax when I can hear imaginary crickets chirping in cyber-space.

In the meantime, I've got more columns to write, more Placentia readers to meet and more adventures to experience and share. And if I need direction, I'll just ask, what would Erma do?

## LISTEN TO THE MUSIC

One of the many things I think I'll get to every summer is to attend one of the Concerts in the Park. I usually go on our city's website to find out which group will be playing what style of music every week, and picture myself and my family on a blanket, having a cool drink, listening to music on a warm summer night.

And yet, in all my years in Placentia, I've never attended a single concert.

Mostly, this is because of my second part-time job of teaching horseback riding lessons. For years, I've had at least one student on Thursday afternoons. This means I am usually leaving the ranch in Chino Hills around six o'clock and driving past the park exactly as the band starts playing.

Why not stop and find a parking place, people suggest. I could meet up with Dale and Marcus.

If you've ever worked with horses in the heat of summer, you know the answer to that question. It's not that I am just sweaty. I have been wandering around the arena, teaching, so I am also dusty. Horses sometimes clear the dirt from their noses by blowing in a kind of sneeze, so I get a little horse snot on my clothes. When I'm not fast enough, they wipe their hay-stained mouths on me.

Do I sound like someone you want to sit next to, even in a park?

This summer, however, the stars aligned. I didn't have any Thursday students. In addition, the city decided to try something new, and offered booths to craft vendors as well as food vendors. Since I had a craft booth at a Heritage Day Festival two years ago, I received a letter from the city, offering me the opportunity to sell my books.

It was a win-win. I signed up for four of the eight concerts.

The first Thursday taught me a lot. Marcus helped me set up my booth. The first thing I learned was that he doesn't read my mind and gets a little snarky when I ask him to figure out what I mean by my vague arm gestures and general mumbling.

Next, I learned that bringing extra stuff means schlepping extra stuff, which is more work than it's worth. I didn't rearrange my boxes of books, so I had a lot more inventory than I needed. When I signed up for the booth, I calculated that I'd need to sell four books to break even. I wasn't certain what kind of sales I might have, but I thought four books might be a dream and not a goal.

So why bring a box of fifty?

The most important thing I learned is to keep my car on the premises. Marcus drove my minivan home, then came back at 8 p.m. to pick me up. Unfortunately, they wouldn't let him drive back in until everyone had cleared the park. It was well after nine before we drove home.

The evening itself was wonderful. I met readers, I met members of the City Council, and I met old friends. The music was entertaining and lively, and it felt communal and homey, like some kind of reunion. I sold my four books, but breaking even wasn't as important to me as making connections with my fellow residents.

I won't be back with my booth until July 28, however, I had so much fun at the concert, I think I'll wander down to Tri-City this Thursday with my blanket and some spare cash for kettle corn.

It's a great way to spend a summer evening.

## In Placentia, One Thing Leads to Another

This summer, I enjoyed four glorious Thursday evenings in Tri-City Park. My vendor's booth sat at the top of the hill, giving me a great view of the bands and a place to meet everyone. Although I had hoped to sell enough books to cover the cost of the booth, my real reason for being at the park was to hang out with my friends and neighbors.

I admit, it's not much of a sales tactic.

Each evening was more fun than the last. Not only did I see my friends, readers came by to say hello. I also met members of our City Council, and the Cultural Arts Commission. Everyone was friendly.

One night, Jim Paddock of the Rotary Club introduced himself to me. I was familiar with the Rotary Club—they're the organization the Valencia High School Vocal Jazz group serenades each December at their holiday party. I use the word "party" loosely. It is a breakfast, held at 7 a.m., meaning I was up at 6 a.m. in order to schlep students to and from the event.

No party hats are worn, but they serve a nice breakfast.

Jim asked if I would like to be a guest speaker at their meeting.

"We'd love to hear about your Placentia stories," he said.

Many people are more afraid of public speaking than dying, but I am not one of them.

"Sounds great," I told him. "I'd love to.

That's when he added, "We meet at seven in the morning at the Alta Vista Country Club."

I might have flinched a little when he mentioned the time. I am not a perky woman in the morning, and often cannot put one foot in front of the other, let alone string coherent words into a sentence. I had just agreed to do it, however, so I shoved away visions of oversleeping and showing up in my pajamas, and pumped up my enthusiasm.

"Perfect."

After I coordinated a date with program chairperson Michelle Cummings, she asked if I needed any electronic equipment. I told her I was fairly self-contained, and prepared my twenty minute talk by writing down some key points. I also prayed for lots of coffee.

On the morning of the meeting, my prayers were answered. Jim handed me a cup of hot caffeine as I walked into the room and Michelle ushered me to a seat. The meeting was more upbeat and fun than most. No one argued over anything, or droned on about something boring.

It wasn't like anything I experienced as an engineer.

After breakfast and a song and nothing but good news reported, I got up and told them about being an accidental resident of Placentia. A new house enticed me to move here from Fullerton in 1984, and three homes later, I'm still in town.

I explained the need to leave my engineering career in order to be a more supportive mom to our son and they nodded. I teased Deputy Police Chief Ward Smith about my habit of peppering the city with a few dead bodies in my mysteries and he smiled.

At least, I think that was a smile and not a grimace.

In the end, I hope I made it clear to everyone that I may have started out as an accidental resident in Placentia, but I've grown to be one of its many cheerleaders.

They were an appreciative group and even donated a book in my name to the Placentia Library. I sold a couple of my books, too, but that wasn't important.

I was there to hang out with my friends and neighbors.

## OF HERITAGES AND REMEMBRANCES

There's a John Lennon song, *Beautiful Boy*, that says "Life is what happens to you while you're busy making other plans." That line and the song have never been as fitting to me as they were this past week.

Last spring, the Placentia Heritage Committee sent me an invitation to have a booth for my books at this year's festival. Two years ago, I applied for a booth and had to wait to see if they thought selling my book was appropriate for a craft vendor. I must have passed their test, because now I am invited.

This year I would have three books available, so I was very excited to get the letter from them, and signed up immediately.

It was going to be a glorious October for me, and the Placentia Heritage Festival would be the icing on my very tasty cake. Whether or not I sold books didn't matter as much as being part of the festivities and meeting people.

Everything was packed and my plans were set.

On Tuesday prior to the big day, life happened. We got news that a dear friend died. It was a huge shock to everyone, since Jeremy was only 33 and in supposedly good health. We have been friends with his family for years and have watched him grow up, which made it less like losing a friend and more like losing a nephew.

My heart sank when I saw the announcement for the memorial service. It was to be Saturday at eleven o'clock in Temecula. I wanted to be at the memorial. It was also important to be at the park. I had told people I would be there, and there was no way to explain an empty booth space to anyone.

Marcus came to my rescue via Facebook. He sent me a message, "Want me to work the booth?"

At first, I hesitated. My son is not shy, but he's also not outgoing. He's also never read any of my books. Could he sell them?

I quickly dismissed my doubts. My college son, already saddled with work, could justifiably stick his nose in his books and ignore my plight. But he didn't. He volunteered to come home for the weekend, get up at six in the morning to help me set up the booth, then sit behind a table and try to sell books.

How could I refuse?

With Marcus in my thoughts, Dale and I drove down to the memorial service. It was a mixture of extreme tears and extreme laughter, as friends and family shared their stories of a much-loved young man. One theme emerged: Jeremy made everyone feel like they were his best friend, and no party could ever start until they were there.

After the service, we drove home and Dale dropped me off at the park, where I promptly handed Marcus money and sent him in search of food. He returned with sandwiches, drinks, kettle corn, and more sandwiches.

Turns out, he hadn't eaten all day.

"I sold six books," he told me. "People kept coming by and saying, 'Are you Marcus? I read about you all the time.' I don't know what to say to people when they tell me that."

"You're supposed to tell them it's lies," I said.

We had a great afternoon, selling more books and talking about random nonsense. I was aware of how much fun I was having with this son of mine. I was also still thinking about Jeremy and his family.

Most of all, I thought about beautiful boys, and how life happens whether we plan it or not.

## HERE SHE IS...

As a girl growing up, I did not care for all the frilly dresses my mother bought me. I preferred my play clothes, and wanted to go outdoors and climb trees. Unfortunately, I was a sickly child and had to stay inside a lot.

I was still a tomboy in my dreams.

As you can guess, this did not make me a fashion maven, nor did it make me look forward to watching the Miss America pageant. I did not want a crown and didn't care who else might get one.

In time, I became a little more interested in the competition. A friend of mine won Miss Orange County, and although I didn't envy her the gowns or the crown or the endless weeks of dieting and spray tans, I did respect what she was doing.

I even stopped calling it the Teeth and Legs Contest.

So when Kathi Baldwin approached me at one of the Concerts in the Park this summer and asked if I would be a judge at the Miss Placentia/Yorba Linda pageant, I said yes. Actually, I asked if the job came with a crown.

She said no, but I still agreed to do it.

In December, I received a package in the mail. Thirteen resumes and thirteen essays were inside, with instructions on what to do, and rules about how to do it.

At that time, I found out I would be judging the Miss Outstanding Teen pageant. I read all the rules, which were very serious and quite daunting. The Teen pageant falls under the same guidelines as Miss America, and everything is done to make it fair and square.

During the week before the contest, I read the resume and essay of each girl and crafted questions for the interview. I had no idea of how many I was going to ask or what kind of answers to expect, but the instructions said to generate questions based on their interests, so that's what I did.

I was not about to disobey any of the rules.

On Saturday morning, I met with the other judges and our lovely coordinator, who explained everything to me and told me I was going to be great at this. It's a good thing one of us thought that.

Our first contestant came in the door and the other judges began asking questions.

"What can you tell us about the Presidential elections?"

Wait—that wasn't on their resumes. You mean I could ask about things that aren't on their resumes? I didn't read that in the rules.

I quickly learned the girls should know about current events, and I needed to step up and jump into the question fray. If I waited for a lull in the action, I'd never ask anyone anything.

Eventually, I got into the rhythm of the interviews and the morning flew by. We ate lunch, then retired to the Valencia High School Auditorium for the rest of the event.

The experience was intense. We couldn't speak to anyone and we were sequestered during intermission. I saw one of my friends in the audience and was afraid to make eye contact, in case someone accused me of signaling in Morse code using my eyelids.

At the end of it all, we chose Miss Outstanding Teen Placentia and Yorba Linda. All of the young ladies were truly remarkable, and the other judges were so friendly, I hated to see the day end. I'd be a judge again in a heartbeat. I wouldn't even need a crown.

I would like a tiara, though.

## I CAN'T SAY NO TO MY CITY

When I worked as a software engineer, I had to fit the rest of my life around when projects were due. This made things like marriage, motherhood, and household chores difficult. Volunteer work was impossible.

No one really wanted my ten available minutes twice a year.

After I left Raytheon, I ventured slowly into Volunteer Land.

First, I helped with Marcus' 6th grade graduation party at Morse Elementary, by turning the activity room into a trip to Hawaii. Then, at Kraemer Middle School, I accompanied his GATE class to San Francisco.

Trust me, imaginary trips to Hawaii are less stressful than real trips to northern California.

At Valencia, I joined the choir boosters and suddenly found my hand in the air whenever someone asked for volunteers. They appointed me president in Marcus' senior year, which kept my plate too full to do much else.

Or so I thought. When Mary Weddle asked for volunteers to help with Grad Night, I explained that I really didn't have time for it, and then signed up to sell tickets and decorate the gym.

That was when my volunteer addiction began.

I thought about my early forays into 6th grade graduation parties and high school booster clubs last week, as I sat at the Placentia Library and listened to the stories of three remarkable women.

For twenty years, (Anna C.) Pat Irot, (Patricia) Pat Jertberg, and Marie Schmidt volunteered their time to collect and categorize items for the Placentia Library History Room. They all began their work together, as strangers. Last Monday night, they all officially retired together, as friends.

I admire these women for being able to work together in that small room for such a long time. I don't know of many marriages that would survive working that closely together.

After all, wedding vows promise "in sickness and in health." Hot flashes are not mentioned.

When I volunteered my services to the Placentia Library, I wondered where they would use me. I'm glad it wasn't the History Room, as my family always tells me that I do not remember the past. This is why I keep clogging the garbage disposal with potato skins.

Actually, I was very good at history in school, even if I was easily distracted by quirky facts. I don't remember beans about Charlemagne, but I can tell you how to ride an elephant and why the 45-caliber pistol was invented.

The people at the library must have sensed I would not be a good fit for the History Room, so they turned me over to the Friends Foundation. This is the group who raises money to pay for programs at the library, like the Summer Reading Program and the Computer Lab.

They really should have looked at my monthly budgeting before they asked me to fundraise.

I've mostly spent my time attending meetings and trying to give ideas and opinions without being bossy. Last year, I was on the Author's Luncheon committee. I did a few clerical duties and helped get a nice article in the paper, but I didn't do nearly as much as everyone else. I complained afterward that they didn't give me enough tasks, so this year they put me in charge of the luncheon.

That should teach me a lesson.

Now that my plate is full of preparing for the library's biggest yearly fundraiser, I was asked by my local Sisters in Crime organization to be their secretary. I don't really have time to do it, so of course I said yes.

I may need an intervention. Any volunteers?

# JUDGING VALENCIA'S TALENT IS NOT EASY

When Marcus left Valencia High School, I said a tearful good-bye. Not only was he was shaped significantly by his teachers and advisors there, I was welcomed as a parent and felt like part of the team. The school will always have a special place in my heart.

So imagine my delight when I was asked to be a judge at their annual Talent Show. After being a judge at the Miss Outstanding Teen Placentia/Yorba Linda Competition, I was thrilled to be giving my fair and impartial opinion to these young people.

I didn't even mind being asked at the last minute, as a replacement for a judge who had to cancel.

The Talent Show was started at VHS years ago, but had been suspended for a few years. It returned in full force the year Marcus was a senior. I still remember some of the acts. There were great singers, musicians, and dancers, and I couldn't imagine how the judges could pick a winner.

To my surprise, Marcus and his two friends from band won with their jazz combo. I thought they were good, but I'm no judge of my son's abilities. After all, I'm his mom. My DNA requires me to love everything he does.

As a judge, I was instructed to be there a half an hour before the program began. I decided to walk over, instead of drive, since the school is mere blocks from our house. It all felt familiar, like being a choir parent again.

Walking into the auditorium was like going home. I can't count the hours I spent there, listening to concerts, and running errands during rehearsals. I probably brought them more pizza and sandwiches than a delivery service. At the time, it felt like I was always trying to stay ahead of all the different tasks, like juggling an apple, a chainsaw, and a cat.

I had forgotten how much fun it was.

When I arrived, they were still trying to run through lighting, curtain, and microphone cues. Megan Arthurton, the choir director, was trying to get everything accomplished so she could open the doors to the audience.

The completion of tasks and opening of the house converged just before everyone lost all patience. It felt so normal, I got a little sentimental.

Once the audience was seated, the evening began. I sat with my score sheet and my fellow judges, Assistant Principal Rick Lopez and Mrs. Arthurton's husband, Noel, who also ran the sound booth for the night. I listened to the first performer, a singer. She was very good. So was the next one. So were the dancers, the pianist, the girl who did the monologue, and the magician.

There were twenty-five acts, and all were all delightful, in their own ways. I found my score sheet covered in notes and numbers. How was I going to choose a winner from this bunch?

The vocal jazz group sang two songs while the three of us deliberated. We had all used different scoring methods to come up with our top three, but were very close in our final selections. There was a brief discussion of how to define talent for the purpose of this show. Were we looking for the raw talent to sing on key, or were we looking for a total package of skill and entertainment?

In the end, we selected three deserving acts out of the many wonderful performances. I wish we could have named them all winners.

I confess, part of me also wishes Marcus was still at high school. It's good to have a little crazy in your life.

## MY TURN AT THE AUTHOR'S LUNCHEON HELM

Those winds you felt blowing through Placentia on March 3rd weren't the Santa Anas. They were collective sighs of relief from the Placentia Library staff and the Friends Foundation. The annual 2012 Author's Luncheon was over.

The Author's Luncheon is the biggest fundraiser of the year for the library, held at the Alta Vista Country Club. A lot of work is done to entice people to come, have a good time, and raise money for our library programs.

All in all, I think it was a success. Everyone had a great time and nothing fell apart.

Last year, I was on the Author's Luncheon committee. I showed up at meetings, performed a few little tasks, but felt I hadn't truly participated. Afterward, I mentioned this to our PLFF President. She smiled at me.

Then she asked me to be in charge of it.

At first, I was completely daunted and made everyone pinky-swear they would help me, which of course, they said they would. We began having monthly meetings, where we went over a list of duties. The list had been handed down to me from the previous chairperson. It was all very organized.

It occurred to me that running the Author's Luncheon was not much different than the Valencia High School choir's Dinner Theater, except that we didn't have to find a caterer. We only had to find an author or two.

Lucky for me, I know a lot of authors now that I am one. We did send out requests for some rather famous names, but they wanted to charge a fee for speaking. I understand the need to pay for costs such as food, but I'm not fond of paying speakers to raise money for a nonprofit organization.

Call me crazy, but I think fundraisers are supposed to raise funds.

Two of my author friends who are mystery writers volunteered to come and speak, and our theme, Make Mine a Mystery, was born. The committee had a great time with the decorations and advertising.

As we approached the date, there were daily fires to be quenched, ads to be placed, and press releases to be written. Through it all, I counted on the members of the committee to tell me where to go and what to do. They were happy to do it—and they were kind.

On the day of the luncheon, everything went smoothly. Everything except that a bunch of people called at the last minute wanting tickets and we said yes. We normally don't take money at the door, nor do we accept walk-ins. But the Alta Vista Country Club staff said they could handle extras, and even set up more tables in order to feed them.

How could we turn away more donors?

To add to the merriment, one of the authors was driving from San Diego and texted me an hour before the event that she was stuck in traffic because of an accident on the I-5. I smiled and kept my fingers crossed. She arrived in plenty of time.

As the luncheon progressed, people had to keep reminding me that I was supposed to be somewhere else, doing something else. I popped up and down from my table so much, I must have looked like a jack-in-the-box.

Afterward, I spoke to a couple of the committee members, thanking them and planning one more meeting to go over lessons learned. I said we should pass these on to whoever chairs the luncheon next year.

They both just looked at me and smiled. I wonder what that means.

# THE HIGH PRICE OF WANDERING

I love being in Placentia. It's true, I do wander off to other places, but most of all, I love to be home. I like my neighborhood and the lovely people who live here. And I suspect karma punishes me whenever I venture too far away for too long.

Sometimes I come home to an insect invasion, even though I make certain the kitchen is clean and all trash is removed before I leave. We have returned to ants in the cat food, and flies in the windows for no apparent reason.

Coming home to a mess that needs immediate cleanup feels like I never went on vacation at all. I expect to unload suitcases and do laundry, but I expect to do that eventually, not as soon as I hit the door. It's hard to ignore the cat's pleas for a dish of food that's not moving, and as for the flies, they just have to go.

I can't relax with all that buzzing.

Sometimes karma slaps me the day after I come home. Last week, I went to Del Mar to compete in a horse show on Thursday and Friday, then joined Dale in Oceanside for a jazz festival on Saturday. Marcus was singing at the festival (with the Cal State Long Beach Jazz & Tonic), as were the Valencia High School vocal jazz group, so we got to see a lot of people we knew.

Due to the nature of horse shows and my unwillingness to pay for one more night at a hotel, I drove to Del Mar and back one day, then drove down and stayed for the remainder of the week.

My 15-year old minivan is still capable of the trip; however, it has an ongoing problem. There is a little device that is supposed to help reduce the emissions, and it keeps getting clogged. My mechanic, Allen, keeps cleaning it out, but it gets clogged again. When it does, the "Service Engine Soon" light pops on.

On the second trip down to Del Mar, the light came on. I knew it wasn't serious, so I figured I'd take the van in on Monday to be unclogged.

I had a fun time at the horse show, worked hard, had some great meals with good friends, and even won a couple of blue ribbons. Then I went to Mira Costa College and sat in a comfy chair all day Saturday, listening to vocal jazz groups. I drove home on Sunday morning, preparing my schedule for the week. There was laundry, grocery shopping, and car repair, all in a general order. I also had an appointment for a baseline bone density scan.

Then I got a text from Marcus. "Totes forgot to mention my car window fell off the tracks." ('Totes' is apparently the abbreviation for 'totally' in teen-speak.)

My clogged device suddenly took a back seat to a window that wouldn't stay up. I arranged for Marcus to get his car to our house, then spent Monday and Tuesday driving back and forth to Allen's shop and Cal State Long Beach. The rest of my schedule was squeezed in around taking care of my son.

I did manage to keep my appointment for my scan. It was the easiest test I've ever taken. I hope I passed.

By Wednesday, all of my rearranging seemed to be done. The laundry is still in progress, and I have enough food to keep us from starving. As far as my car's repair goes, well, I guess I'll try that next Monday.

After all, I'm staying in Placentia this weekend.

## COWABUNGA! WHAT A LOT OF CRABS!

When I first moved to southern California, all the little cities that made up Orange County looked pretty much alike to me. If I was at the beach, I couldn't tell if it was Newport or Huntington. If I was inland, I didn't know Brea from Buena Park.

I recognized Disneyland, but that doesn't count as a city.

Even after moving to Placentia, I confess I wasn't as aware as I should have been of the things that make it stand out from its neighbors. I suppose I was young, new to the area, and too busy discovering where life was going to take me. It took thirty years for me to get to know this town.

Forgive me, Placentia. I'm sorry I ignored you.

Last week showed me a glimpse of how far I've come, when Dale and I attended the Placentia Rotary Club's Cowabunga Crabfest. I had heard about the fundraiser through the library, as well as from my friends on Facebook.

When I was younger, I might have said no to this event, thinking that I wouldn't know anyone. Now that I'm older, I bought two tickets as soon as I heard about it. After all, I'm not as shy as I used to be. I'll talk to anyone who comes within speaking distance.

If no one's around, I just talk to myself.

On Saturday, I ran home from the ranch, cleaned up a little, and drove with Dale to Kraemer Memorial Park. We had to park on Bradford Avenue and walk, which was a little difficult for Dale, since he injured his Achilles tendon and was using a cane. Usually I'm rushing to keep up with my husband, so it was weird to find myself ten paces ahead of him and having to back up to walk by his side.

We got our plates of crab, with coleslaw and corn and went looking for a place to sit. There was an open table in a shady spot so we sat our plates down. I looked around and saw a familiar face—Gae Wood, whom I know from the library. She waved me over.

"Don't sit by yourselves, we can squish together," she told me as she rearranged her chairs.

We squeezed our plates in among a crowd of people who liked to chat and eat. As the afternoon progressed, even more folks joined us. Pretty soon our table reminded me of late nights at the writers conferences I attend, where there's always room for one more chair at the table, until the entire room is one big group.

I felt right at home.

Many at the table, including myself, had only cracked open crab legs, and didn't know how to open and eat the meat in the body. Good thing Dale is an expert. It was fun to have my hubby show everyone how to use the hammer and then pry the meat from the underside.

We saw a lot of people we knew, and met people we didn't. I sat next to a fascinating man who is originally from Hungary, shared a few jokes with Al and Gloria Shkoler, and even saw our neighbors, the Saucedas. Scott and Robin Nelson dropped by our table to say hello, and our mayor, Jeremy Yamaguchi, was running around behind the scenes, working with the sound equipment.

When I was a little girl, I used to watch "The Andy Griffith Show" and thought it would be fun to live in a town where everyone was so friendly. Who knew I'd find such a place in the middle of southern California?

## When tragedy hits one small town, it hits us all

The longer I live in Placentia, the more I love our town, in that fierce, stubborn way that Dale loves the Lakers whether they are winning or losing. Our city is not perfect but we try to reward what's best and correct what's wrong.

And whether our little village is winning or losing, I'm still glad to be here, cheering it on.

When tragedy hit Newtown, Connecticut two weeks ago, I was as devastated as everyone else. A disturbed resident took out his unexplained rage on innocent lives in his own town. In ten minutes, one horrible act had destroyed a community.

I thought back to all of Marcus' years in Morse Elementary, then Kraemer Middle School, and on to Valencia. Each school spent time each year strengthening their security procedures. They built fences and practiced drills and sent home announcements to tell us what to do in an emergency.

Now I ask myself, were we really safe or just lucky?

The day of the shooting, Marcus was singing The Messiah in a church choir in San Pedro. He had given me the information, but I had not intended to go. It was Friday, and it was raining. San Pedro might as well be on the other end of the universe from Placentia.

After I read the news that day, I knew I had to see my son.

It took me an hour and a half to drive thirty-five miles to the Holy Trinity Church. I managed to go in the wrong door, then found my way to the table to leave a donation and pick up a program.

This was a Catholic church, and I was raised as a Baptist, so I took a seat toward the back and hoped I would not commit any liturgical faux-pas during the evening. A very short woman sat down beside me and started the conversation by saying she hoped she could see over everyone's heads.

I gestured to the books that were stuffed in the racks on the back of the pew. "You could always sit on those," I offered.

She liked that idea and had soon stacked them under her tush. "This is better," she said.

We exchanged opinions about the traffic and weather. When I told her why I had driven from Placentia, she held out her program and asked which one was my son. I pointed to Marcus' name.

"You can't miss him. He's got the biggest hair."

I was right. She recognized him right away.

The music was beautiful and uplifting and comforted me almost as much as watching my son singing it. And when we all stood for the Hallelujah Chorus, I felt a sense of community, even with these strangers in a strange town.

At the end of the concert, I moved to the center aisle to greet Marcus as he walked past. He stopped and hugged me. I tried to play it cool, but I couldn't help hugging him a little too tightly.

"I love you, too, Mom," he said.

We had a brief conversation before he had to run off to a party. I wanted to stay and talk longer. I had even hoped to take him to dinner, then remembered he had mentioned the party earlier.

But in the end, it was okay. I got to see him, hug him, and talk to him. I could go home happy.

But just because my son is safe doesn't mean that I can relax. I'm going to roll up my sleeves and help Placentia where I can. This is my community.

## EVEN CELEBRITIES KNOW US

When I was appointed to the Trustee position at the Placentia Library last June, I had to resign from the Placentia Library Friends Foundation board. Still, there was one task that I told the PLFF I would complete. Last year, when I was in charge of our yearly Author's Luncheon, I had written to Dean Koontz to see if he was available.

I felt a little bold to ask someone so famous to come speak at our little library function, but if you never ask, the answer is always no.

Mr. Koontz wrote back that he was completely booked for 2012, but if we would like him to come in 2013, he could do that. I don't know whether he's just a gracious man, or if he's really so humble, he thinks our interest in him is a passing fancy, but it didn't matter. I immediately took him up on his offer.

Now, a year later, I will complete my PLFF duties by being their liaison to our author for this year's luncheon.

I confess, as March 2nd approached, I found myself more and more nervous about Mr. Koontz's appearance. He had signed the contract and I have heard that he is an honorable man, so I knew he planned to be there.

However, I went to see him at the Fullerton Library this past year, hoping to get a book signed and actually meet him. He had to leave early due to a last-minute scheduling conflict, but he did pre-sign books and give them to us.

Still, I didn't want any scheduling conflicts for our luncheon.

It didn't ease my mind that every time I called him to get some questions answered about his visit, he wasn't in and I had to leave a message. Was he bringing an entourage for us to feed at the luncheon? Was he a vegetarian? Would he stay to sign books?

Imagine my relief when he called me back this week. Forget my relief; imagine my attempt to stay calm and business-like.

I don't know why the man is like a rock star to me, except that he is such a famous and prolific author and I aspire to be even half as successful in my writing as he is. At any rate, in my attempt not to squeal in his ear like a crazed fan, I think my voice dropped an octave. I asked him how he was, just to buy time to find the paper with all my questions and step outside.

He had called my cell phone, which seems to hate my house and drops calls without warning. There was no way I was going to lose this call.

I asked my questions in a low, slightly shaking voice and hoped I sounded sane. He answered as if he was now wondering what he'd signed up for. When I asked about his meal, he replied that he was happy to provide company at whoever's table, but he had learned long ago not to eat before he spoke.

"Oh, you'll be at my table," I told him. "The seating for this luncheon is assigned. I'll be your assistant for the day."

I'm not certain whether this made him feel better or more nervous.

We ended the call and I did my happy dance around the house. I felt a lot more confident about the luncheon, even if I'm still concerned about controlling my excitement when I meet him.

It's my last hurrah as a member of the PLFF, but I'm not complaining. I just don't want to mess it up.

## GRADUATING FROM TEEN TO QUEEN

I may be a woman of a certain age, but I still like to learn new things. A saying that has always stuck with me is, "When you're green, you're growing, and when you think you're ripe, you're rotten."

Still, I'm always surprised when one little thing results in a big change.

Last year, I got the opportunity to judge the Miss Outstanding Teen competition for Placentia and Yorba Linda. I expected some stress as I reviewed the contestants' resumes, but I never imagined how tense I would feel, trying to choose the right young women.

Naturally, when they asked me to judge Miss Placentia/Yorba Linda this year, I said yes. I live for pressure.

Prior to the Miss Outstanding Teen contest, I had jokingly requested a tiara from Executive Director Kathi Baldwin. She said no, which was okay, since I really didn't want a tiara.

That is, until I got one.

My friend Tameri gave me a large, sparkly tiara when I was appointed trustee of the Placentia Library. It's hefty and has combs to keep it attached to my head. Over the summer, I wore it at the Concerts in the Park, much to the delight of the crowned Miss Outstanding Teens.

By the time the 2013 pageant rolled around, I realized something: I'm hooked on bling.

I never needed rhinestones or sparkles before. My competition shirts for horse shows have both, and I used to joke that after showing, I planned to go sing some Patsy Cline numbers at the karaoke bar.

Now I'm wondering if they're shiny enough.

When I got dressed for the day of judging, I looked around my closet for something sparkly. I didn't have anything, and my western shirts would not be appropriate, so I chose basic black and wore some big silver jewelry instead. After one longing gaze at my tiara in its red velvet box, I left.

This year there were only nine young ladies, but the day was still stressful. They had spent four months training for this day, and only two of them would go on to compete at the state level. How could I pick the right two?

Thank goodness there were six other judges to help me.

The morning's interviews showed me how these girls handled random questions being thrown at them. I imagined myself as a young woman in front of seven adults and wondered where I would find the courage.

I'd have been shaking in my three-inch heels.

After a lovely dinner at El Farolito, I joined the judges at the Valencia High School Auditorium for the evening competition. The girls were radiant in their gowns, confident in their swimsuits, and diverse in their talents. My job should have been easy. After all, I was choosing two winners out of an entire group of fabulous young women. How hard could that be?

As I cast my final vote, I briefly wished for my tiara. Wearing it might not give me the right answers, but at least I'd look good while I decided.

After the winners were crowned, I said my goodbyes and went home to slip into my pajamas and pour a glass of wine. I had done my best to be decisive, to think about what it takes to represent Placentia and Yorba Linda, and which young women could carry that responsibility on their shoulders.

There was a post-pageant reception at the Yorba Linda Country Club, but I declined. I felt too exhausted to drive to a country club and mingle. Besides, I had left my tiara at home.

## PARDON MY FANGIRL MOMENT

I'm trying to remain coherent for this column, but I'm afraid it's hard to get my head out of the clouds and my feet back in reality. Last Saturday, I met Dean Koontz.

Two years ago, I wrote him a letter to see if he would speak at our Placentia Library Friends Foundation Author's Luncheon. Ordinarily, I am not a crazy fan-girl, but when he wrote me back, I was suddenly star struck.

Earlier in the year, I spoke with him on the phone and went over a few of the details. That went well, so I thought we were all set for Saturday.

I envisioned waiting for his limo to pull up at the Alta Vista Country Club, extending my hand and saying, "Hello, Mr. Koontz, I'm Gayle Carline." Afterward, we would sit at the table and discuss the craft of writing.

A week before the luncheon, I got a phone call. It was from Dean's chief of security, wanting to see the venue and go over the program with me. Suddenly, I felt like a secret agent, making plans with him to case the joint.

When I mentioned this to some people, they scoffed. Why would Dean Koontz need security? Because he is a famous author who writes thrillers about fictional scary, violent bad guys, and he's received threats from actual scary, violent bad guys.

The security chief assured me that while they were there to protect Mr. Koontz, they weren't there to obstruct the fun of our luncheon. He was correct. When Saturday arrived, there was lots of fun and no obstructions.

Of course, nothing went the way I had planned it in my head, either.

The first thing we always do at the luncheon is take a picture of the author with the library trustees, PLFF board members and other city officials. Jeanette, our library director, herded us all into chairs in the lobby ahead of time so we could be ready for Mr. Koontz.

My vision of meeting him at the curb evaporated. Security met him instead and ushered him to the lobby. They introduced me and I convinced him to sit in the empty chair next to mine for the photograph.

After that, everyone found their tables, then milled about until it was time to start the program. I was a celebrity waiter, so I rounded up coffee and iced tea for my table.

Jeanette and her cohorts presented a skit to kick off the event, aided by Trustee Board President Al Shkoler and our mayor Scott Nelson. It made everyone laugh.

Lunch was then served. In between trying to help serve food and drinks, I got to sit next to Dean Koontz and talk to him. Did I talk to him about writing?

No. First, I asked him if he writes his own Tweets (he does, but his assistant posts them). Then we discussed our dogs. Before I knew it, it was time for him to speak.

He gave one of the funniest speeches I've heard in a long time, and kept the audience enthralled. Afterward, he answered many questions.

There was some chaos as he took his seat to sign books and people were trying to line up, but eventually we got the whole room back in order and everyone got their books autographed, their photos snapped with Dean and even more questions answered.

I got lots of hugs from everyone for my role in getting him to our event. It felt good, but undeserved. All I did was write him a letter.

## ROTARY CLUB IS A GREAT PLACE FOR STUDENTS

When the Placentia Library Director Jeanette Contreras asked if I would be a judge for a speech competition, I said yes without hesitation. After all, I sat on the panels to pick Miss Placentia and Miss Outstanding Teen, which is a rigorous process. Judging students for scholarship awards should not be a problem.

Then she told me the competition was at the monthly Rotary Club meeting.

I love the Rotary Club. I've visited, as a guest, three times now, not counting the number of times I shuttled members of the Valencia High School Vocal Jazz group to the Rotary's holiday party so they could perform.

The thing is, our Rotary Club meets for breakfast at the Alta Vista Country Club. By breakfast, I mean their meeting starts at 7:00 a.m. While this is within my normal breakfast time, I'm usually fumbling around the kitchen in my pajamas, trying to extract a filter from the container and brew a pot of coffee.

You could say I'm not a morning person. When I worked as an engineer, I woke up at 6:00 every morning because I had to get to the office. When Marcus was young, I woke at 6:00 because I had to get him up and off to school. As soon as I no longer had to do either of those things, my body rejected 6:00 a.m. as wake-up time.

But Jeanette and the Rotary Club needed me to be there at 6:50, so I rose to the occasion. Literally.

I had selected some clothes the evening before so I wouldn't have to make any tough decisions in the morning. Getting the contact in my left eye was a little tricky, since neither eye cared to open fully, but I managed it, then slapped on some makeup and brushed my hair. I actually arrived early.

As usual, I was greeted by old friends who offered me a seat, and more importantly, coffee. It took two cups to get my eyes to stop squinting like a mole in sunshine. I was joined by the other judges, Mayor Scott Nelson, and PYLUSD School Board Trustee Judi Carmona. It's always a pleasure to sit and chat with them.

The meeting was lively and fun. We got our breakfast, then sat down and prepared to listen. There were nine names listed on the program, but only three teens were there for the event. The topic for the speeches was "Peace Through Service."

I was impressed by the poise and confidence of these young people. They each made the topic their own, promoting their ideas of how to achieve peace by serving others, using language that was well-developed without being too sophisticated for a teenager.

It's easy to look at the young person walking down the street with their earbuds and cellphone and think that the world will be inherited by the self-absorbed. But hearing these teens reminded me that there is great hope for the future. Each one spoke of helping the world by helping the community. They all recognized the ability to make a difference at the grass-roots level.

It was a difficult decision, but we selected a first, second, and third place speech. They were all given checks and the winner will advance to the next level of competition.

Every time I come to a Rotary meeting, someone talks to me about joining. It's such a fine organization, I am always tempted. Then I look at the clock and see that it's 7:30 and I'm in high heels, and I hesitate.

I wonder if they'd let me come to the meetings in my pajamas.

## CONSTRUCTING LEMONADE OUT OF ROADWORK LEMONS

In my continuing attempts to get from my house to anywhere in Orange County, I've decided that historians will someday refer to these years as the Construction Era. Books will be written about the sociological impact of concrete barricades. Essays will be posted about the philosophy behind the 'Detour' sign. Perhaps they'll even put orange cones and caution tape on display in a museum.

These days, I'm just doing my best to find an alternate route to anywhere.

The project on Kraemer Boulevard has been taking forever, and does not look like it will end soon. I've been without a straight route to Orangethorpe Avenue for such a long time now, I may have a permanent blind spot. Even when it opens, I'll still be turning down Chapman or winding my way around Melrose because I think there are still barricades on Kraemer.

The only bright spot so far is the flashing sign warning me that "Kreamer is closed ahead." I always wonder if there's any "koffee" to go with that.

Recently, I walked down to the Placentia Library to get my agenda for the Trustee meeting, and discovered that the construction crew had extended their domain to the pedestrian world. Every corner on Kraemer was blocked by cones and tape, causing me to walk into the street to get around. Fortunately, traffic was light. I'm not a big fan of walking in the same space that cars occupy.

As I wound my way to the library, I was thankful the dogs weren't with me. Steering can be optional with them on the sidewalk. I could just picture them getting tangled, and the three of us dragging pylons down the street.

Later in the day I drove down Kraemer toward the ranch and saw that every corner was torn up. Why? Was it some kind of disease, like Street Corner Curb Rot? Did the construction company get a good deal on supplies at one of those buy-in-bulk stores?

A friend pointed out that his curbs in Fullerton were re-done to adjust the slope for new code requirements. Apparently, Kraemer requires a lot of new slopes.

I may be having a few difficulties driving and walking in Orange County in general, and Placentia in particular, but I'm going to look on the bright side. I'm sure it will all be lovely when it's completed, and my driving and walking will go much faster and smoother.

In the meantime, I'm determined to make lemonade from these lemons. What could we do to make street improvements fun?

Dale loves reality TV, and from the ratings, I think he's not alone. Perhaps we could turn our construction zones into a game show. Couples could race through the city, competing at challenges. We could call it "So You Think You Can Find Your Way Around Placentia."

I'm not sure what we could challenge them with. The restaurants are all good here so there would be no nasty food challenges, and there are no cliffs to jump off, so there's nothing to fear. Maybe they could bungee-jump from the top of the water tower, or see how long they can last in line at El Farolito before they swoon from the aroma.

They couldn't even race very fast. They're in a construction zone.

Maybe we could just change our motto to "Placentia: A Pleasant Place to Detour." After all, it's a great city, no matter how long it takes you to drive through it.

## ADVICE FOR EVERYONE, EVEN MYSELF

I saw on Facebook recently that Placentia Yorba Linda School Board Trustee Judi Carmona will be speaking at a couple of high school graduations and she was seeking words of wisdom from friends.

"What's the best piece of advice ever given to you?" she asked.

I read a lot of good advice in the comments of her post, about making a difference and following your bliss. Judi's friends were saying things I wished someone had said to me as a graduating senior.

Actually, people probably did say all those things to me and more, but I was a little preoccupied with wondering what I was going to do tomorrow, and how I was going to turn all those tomorrows into the rest of my life. As an 18-year-old, I'm certain I heard, "Blah, blah, blah, life. Live it."

In my youth, I did stumble upon a magnificent motto. The movie "Auntie Mame" was on TV and I heard the following line: "Life is a banquet and most poor suckers are starving to death." This accounts for my forays into being an artist, an engineer, and a writer, and all of the hobbies I've tried, from knitting to scuba diving to horses.

It's possible I confused the word 'banquet' with 'buffet.'

Some parents might not like it if their children were encouraged to treat life like a Las Vegas all-you-can-eat buffet line. They'd like Junior to focus, choose a college major, get on with his career, and move out of their house.

Later in my life, I discovered a lovely quote from my hero, Erma Bombeck. She said, "When I stand before God at the end of my life, I would hope that I would not have a single bit of talent left, and could say, 'I used everything you gave me'."

It sounds like a perfect way to live your life, but I doubt if 18-year-olds are thinking about the end of their lives. They're barely thinking beyond the end of the week.

There is one piece of advice I'd like to give all graduates, advice that will serve them better than any version of reaching for the stars. It's advice I would like to give everyone under the age of, say, twenty-five.

My advice is, don't look to the internet to solve all of your problems. Nothing beats human interaction.

I've tried to give Marcus this advice, but this week he was really listening.

He called me, slightly panicked. One of the boys has a cat in their apartment, and suddenly, they have fleas. My son has led a sheltered, flea-free life, thanks to my efforts behind the scenes at home.

"They're biting me," he moaned. "I looked it up on Google and it told me to deep clean the carpets and wash the walls and the curtains, and, I don't know, boil water or something."

"No, no, forget Google," I told him. "Go to the pet store. Get something to put on the cat, like flea powder or medicine. Then get some flea bombs."

"Flea what?"

"Bombs. B-O-M-B-S."

Marcus was quiet. It's possible my son thought I was some kind of terrorist.

"Go to the pet store. Tell them your problem. They will help you."

It was nice to see my advice being used, by at least one grad. He got his problem solved, but not by the internet. He went out and asked real people for help. Of course, first, he searched through the Mom database. That will never change.

## SHOWING THAT LOVIN' FEELING FOR PLACENTIA

I think it's easy for us to say we love things. That's not to say that we love them equally. We love our families, but we also love a cold drink on a hot day. Both are legitimate. Love is not a one-size-fits-all feeling.

So when I tell you I love Placentia, you might wonder how much. Do I love it as much as my family, or more like a cold drink?

Well, I might not do as much for my hometown as I would for my family, but this week I think I showed my love in a very concrete way. I attended the Citizen of the Year breakfast.

If I haven't said it enough, I'll repeat myself. I am not a morning person. Back when I was a software engineer, I endured the early hours. On most days, managers wanted me at work by 8 a.m. This wouldn't have been a big problem, except they wanted me to be dressed as well.

I still can't believe I got myself into pantyhose at 7 a.m. five days a week for twenty years.

These days, I only get up early if I have to drive to a horse show, in which case I don't have to do much except slip into jeans and a tee-shirt, and slap on some mascara. I'm still cranky about being awake so early, but at least I have less to be cranky about.

When I was invited as a Library Trustee to the awards breakfast, I confess I was relieved that couldn't make it. The breakfast started at 7:15 and I had to be at the ranch that day before 9 a.m. Then two things happened: my morning lesson cancelled and I spoke with Judi Carmona.

"You're going to be at the breakfast aren't you?" she asked. "I want to talk about your books."

How could I refuse a Placentia Yorba Linda Unified School District board member? Marcus may no longer be a PYLUSD student, but I still feel the urge to be in good standing with the district.

I'm kidding. Judi is not such an imposing member of the board that I was compelled to obey her. She's just a really nice woman, and it made me feel special for her to ask me to come.

So I contacted the library two days before the breakfast. Was it too late for me to attend? The answer was, of course, no. When it comes to honoring our citizens, our motto is the more, the merrier.

On the morning of the event, I rose early and managed to put myself together, including wearing a skirt, and makeup. I even wore a red blouse to make me look awake. Fortunately, they had placed the coffee near the door at the country club. One cup opened my eyes and helped me remember everyone's names.

The breakfast was lovely. I was surrounded by my fellow trustees and the library director. The presentations were all wonderful, particularly the awards given to our police, fire, and emergency services personnel. These are folks that work hard every day to make certain Placentia residents are safe.

How much do I love Placentia? Like my family, I'll defend her from any attackers, and I'll always treat her with respect. But getting up early to honor her?

For me, that's above and beyond.

## MEASURING THE SIZE OF A SMALL TOWN

I recently had an online promotion for one of my mysteries, and my online friends were kind enough to share the information with their friends. I have learned this is the new way of marketing anything. You use social media to spread the word.

It's like that old TV commercial where some girl used a shampoo, then told her friend, who told a friend, and so on, until apparently all the world's hair was lathered.

In my marketing material, I had included the description of the book, which begins, "No one in the small town of Placentia, California is surprised when Benny Needles' house catches fire."

One of my friend's friends posted a comment about the book. I will not embarrass her by using her name, so let's just call her Anonymous Woman. "Anyone been to Placentia, CA?" she asked. "It's not exactly what I call a small town. Over 50,000 residents and a stone's throw from Disneyland. Suburbs maybe, but not a small town."

It was evident to me that, in addition to being snippy, Anonymous Woman is not from southern California. Suburbs, indeed.

I will admit, when I first moved here, all the towns looked alike to me. Decatur, Illinois is my point of origin, and in much of the Midwest, towns are set very far apart, with lots of farmland between each one. When you are in Decatur, when the sidewalk ends, you are literally out to pasture. So it took a little time for me to understand this urban sprawl.

Now I can tell a difference between Placentia, Fullerton, Brea, etc. Each city has its own look, its own hub of activity, even its own set of residents.

Placentia looks like a small town to me. I can walk to the library. When I go to the Concerts in the Park, I see a lot of people I know. In some way, I feel like I can reach out and touch the edges of the town. There may be 50,000 people here, but it feels like maybe 500.

The boundaries do sometimes get hazy sometimes. For years, I thought my local grocery store was in my city. As it turns out, it's in Fullerton. I see a lot of my neighbors in there. Perhaps, like Columbus, we should just stick a flag in the middle of Albertson's and claim it for Placentia.

In an attempt to find out whether I'm the only one to see Placentia as a small town, I threw the question out to a Placentia-centric Facebook group. What did they think?

Almost everyone replied with a resounding "Heck, yes, it's a small town." One lovely woman even looked up the definition of "small town" and proclaimed that 50,000 people fits within the scope of "small." It was great fun to read all their comments about growing up here, and that even if it has changed and grown, it's still their P-Town.

They certainly convinced me not to change my description. It may not be Mayberry, but Placentia is a small town in southern California. And even though my books contain some quirky characters, our residents are nothing but charming and helpful.

## HONORING A LIFE WELL LIVED

One of my favorite quotes is not by anyone famous. It's by a minister who spoke at Dale's grandmother's funeral. He said, "You write your own obituary by the life you lead."

Last week, I went to the memorial service of a woman whose short life left a long epitaph. Pat Hadley had been a teacher and a coach at Valencia High School for many years. I was shocked to hear that she had died in a hiking accident. She was four years younger than me, which made her practically an ingénue in my book.

And yet, her life seemed so full.

She was a world-class mountain bike racer and soccer player, ran marathons, climbed mountains and could do a mean one-handed pushup. But that wasn't the measure of her.

In her ceramics classes, her students were as much works of art to her as their projects. Her job as a track and cross country coach extended beyond teaching kids to run. She taught them to reach for a goal and to not just endure the path to the finish line, but to notice the wildflowers along the way.

And even that doesn't sum up Coach Hadley.

While Marcus was at Valencia, he was on the cross country team for one year. His meets were always when I was teaching at the ranch, so I spoke with Pat a total of maybe three times. I remember exactly two things about her.

First, on at least two occasions when Dale and I could not get Marcus to his meet, she stopped by our house and picked him up. Second, the first time I talked with her, she referred to Marcus as "her Renaissance man."

"He does sports and music and he's a good student, and he kind of just does a little of everything," she explained.

The true measure of her, in my mind, was that after spending so little time with her, I wept when I heard the news. And when I heard the memorial service was going to be held on Friday, I cancelled my appointments and went. I can't imagine someone doing that for me.

There were so many people in the Valencia gymnasium, some stood outside in the foyer. We were all sweating like racehorses from the heat. Everyone was passing around bottles of water. The lady two bleachers down handed me a disposable glove filled with ice cubes. I now owe her a fruit basket. Or a kidney.

The service was uplifting and heartbreaking. Teachers, students, and friends got up to tell stories of all the things Pat had done, both funny and motivational. In everyone's speech, there was the implication that for everything she had done, there was so much more she could have accomplished.

I got the feeling that, no matter when Pat left us, she would have left us too soon.

The service has lingered with me over the past few days. I feel the need to do more, to always have one more goal on the horizon, and to leave people with a good impression. In addition, I wish I could still thank my teachers for what they meant to me. Unfortunately, at my age, not many of them are still alive.

This week, I'd like to make a request. If there's a teacher or a coach who helped you in any way, big or small, write them a note or send them an email. Find a way to thank them. Tell them for Coach Hadley.

## PARADING MY HERITAGE

Placentia Heritage Day is almost here and I'm very excited. In addition to my booth at the festival, I get to ride in the parade.

I wasn't going to talk about it this year. After all, this is my second year to ride in a little motorized train down Kraemer Boulevard. Then I remembered: last year. I was running for office, so my column wasn't in the newspaper.

Now I can give you all the backstage scoop.

For the past few years, I've had a booth at the Heritage Festival in Tri-City Park. I sell my books there, but most important, it's a great way to meet people. Believe it or not, I'm not as outgoing as I seem. Having a booth full of books gives people a reason to chat with me.

When I wander around the park talking to strangers, it usually gives people a reason to call for security.

Last year, I had a problem. I reserved my booth, then received an invitation to ride in the parade, as a library trustee. That meant my booth would be unattended while I was out joyriding.

Still, I couldn't say no. I've never been in a parade before. I spent weeks trying to figure out what to wear and practicing my wave. I settled on a black sequined shirt to go with my tiara.

I know you're wondering about the tiara. My good friend gave it to me. I never knew I wanted one until I put it on. Now, all anyone has to do is dare me to wear it. I can't resist.

Marcus came to my rescue. My little night owl dragged himself from bed and sat in my booth while I drove over to the parade starting line. I wasn't really certain where I was supposed to meet anyone, but that's not unusual.

I always know where I am, even if I don't know where I'm supposed to be.

It didn't take me long to find the other trustees and our director, Jeanette Contreras, along with Clifford the Big Red Dog. We all climbed into the little cars of a brightly-colored train and waited. There was some shuffling about and a few false starts, then we all rolled down the street.

The route is about a mile-and-a-quarter, each way. My first impression of riding in the parade was that I wished I had practiced waving a little more. The repetitive motion tired my arm out quickly. I found myself supporting my right arm at the elbow with my left hand. This not only helped me wave longer, it contained the residual motion from the underside of my bicep.

There was no need for my arm to be waving twice.

My second impression was that the "engineer" of our little train liked to drive erratically. Our cars wound back and forth, then in circles. Just as I began to wave and talk to one group, I would get whipped to the opposite side of the street. I hope the crowds liked the motion more than my stomach did.

Seriously, it was all great fun, followed by an afternoon of talking to lots of people who stopped by my booth to say hi. I'm hoping for the same kind of day this Saturday, although I don't know if Marcus will be filling in at my booth. It is his 21st birthday, so he might have other plans.

At least I'll have my tiara.

## SAYING GOODBYE

Sometimes I think I'm going to write about one thing, and it turns into another. I lost a friend last week, and I had planned to talk about knowing her. Yet after I attended her memorial service, I couldn't help but think about how we say goodbye.

Her name was Gloria Shkoler. She was loved by many and taken too soon. This is the second friend I've lost to pancreatic cancer, and it's two too many. Gloria fought the disease for quite a few years, but not even her strength and optimism could defeat it.

I met Gloria when I started volunteering at the library, which is when I met her husband, Al. I can't say I knew her well, but I always looked forward to seeing her. If you looked up the word "vibrant" in the dictionary, I'm pretty sure you'd find a picture of Gloria. She had a smile for everyone.

And she made you feel like you were great friends, even if all you ever shared was a cup of coffee.

When I saw her at events with Al I thought they looked like the poster couple for How to Have a Happy Marriage. They seemed so compatible.

As soon as I heard the news of her passing, I moved my schedule around so I could attend her service. It was held at the John Paul II Polish Center.

I am not Catholic, although I have attended many events at Catholic churches. Mostly, when I am in a Catholic church, I try to sit still, smile politely, and keep from offending anyone. For the record, I was raised in a Baptist church that was so afraid of any kind of liturgy, we only had communion and baptism.

It's possible we never did those the same way twice.

Gloria's service began with praying the Rosary. It took a very long time to do, and I was mesmerized. After a while, I felt like I knew how to recite along, but refrained, since I didn't want anyone to think I was stepping over my bounds.

The rest of the service was an equally interesting, dignified ritual to celebrate her life. While I didn't join in with everything, I appreciated it all. The Monsignor and Gae Wood added personal words of love for Gloria, which were touching.

Afterward, I thought about all the other services I have attended. Some have been in churches, some in funeral homes. In my family, they consisted of a few songs, a prayer, and a pastor's kind words. During one, the pastor even included an altar call.

When I began to go to services for Dale's family, they were not quite the same. There was a little less music, and after the pastor spoke, friends and family lined up at the altar. One by one, they walked up and said something about the deceased. Usually they told a story, but some just came up and expressed their feelings.

No matter what kind of ceremonial wrappings these events wore, the message was the same. This was a life worth remembering. Usually only the good parts were mentioned. Errors in judgment were edited out.

So here I am, trying to tell you what a generous woman Gloria was, and instead I'm talking about how we say goodbye to our loved ones.

Perhaps I'm talking about the same thing, after all.

## I LOVE A PARADE, AND A CITY

When I moved to Placentia thirty years ago, I had no idea that not only would I become a permanent resident, I'd be a happy one. Until I moved here, I thought where I lived was just an address.

Last Saturday, I got to see a lot of people at the Placentia Heritage Day festivities to remind me how much I enjoy my city.

The day started early. In addition to riding in the parade, I had to set up my booth in Tri-City Park, which meant arriving with my loaded minivan at 6:15. Yes, that is A.M. Everyone knows I am not a morning person. It has to be important for me to step into the shower at 5:00, much less stick a contact lens in my left eye.

Still, I got ready, got there, and got everything set up, then waited for Marcus to arrive. I even brought a box of donut holes to thank him. As soon as he got to the park, I grabbed my tiara and his car keys, and scampered to the parade lineup.

It may be my imagination, but the parade seems to get longer every year. We waited for quite a while before they signaled the library tram to start down the route. Al Shkoler and I represented the trustees in the first car, Yesenia Baltierra from the library and her darling daughter rode in the second car with Clifford the Big Red Dog, and our Summer Reading Celebration winner rode in the last car with their family.

As we waited, a couple of men with horses stood beside our vehicle. The horses seemed pretty calm, which was good because the men were very casual about keeping them in place. At one point, one of the horses turned his tail end toward our car.

Having worked with horses for several years, I admit it made me uncomfortable to be within kicking distance. I was pretty happy when our tram started moving down the street and away from them.

Dale rode with me this year. It was a lot of fun listening to my husband wonder why Clifford was getting all the attention.

"He's a big deal with little readers," I told him.

He also talked about trying out different kinds of waves. "Should I go back and forth or up and down? Maybe I should point."

I spent most of the parade laughing. There were so many families lining Kraemer Boulevard, it was hard to focus on each face. All I could do was keep waving and wish everyone a good morning.

Oh, and graciously accept all the compliments on my tiara.

At the end of the parade, I walked back to my booth and thanked Marcus for getting up so early to help me. The rest of the day was spent talking to people, both friends and strangers. I was thrilled to have a few folks look for my booth to tell me how much they enjoy my column.

My favorite visitor was a man who said he had lived in Fullerton for years. When he moved to Placentia, his sons told him, "That's the kind of town where people drive their cars into the garage on Friday night, close the door, and you don't see them until Monday."

"I've gotten to know this town through your column," he told me.

It may have taken me a few years to fall in love with my city, but now my heart belongs to P-Town.

## When it comes to public speaking, call me crazy

According to studies, public speaking is people's Number One Fear. That places it above dying, which means most folks would rather die than talk to an audience.

I'm not one of those people. Standing in front of a group and talking is as fun for me as it is torture for someone else. And I don't even have to picture everyone in their underwear to do it.

I recently had the opportunity to speak at the Placentia Round Table Women's Club, and I must say, I can't remember when I've had such an enthusiastic audience, or one with more stamina.

When Nancy Melton of the program committee contacted me about speaking, she told me to plan to speak for about 30-40 minutes. I sent her an email, asking her what topic she wanted me to cover. I could discuss how I created the main character for my books, or talk about how I became a writer, or explain why I set my mysteries in Placentia.

"Yes, that would be great," she told me.

Armed with the idea that I'd be covering everything in a half-hour, I spent weeks practicing my talk. Thanks to the late Dr. Enell of Cal State Fullerton who taught speech, I usually don't use notes. I memorized the main points of my beginning, middle, and ending, and rehearsed them a few times.

I was ready.

The meeting began about 9:30 on Wednesday morning with lots of coffee and general conversation among the members. It was called to order at 10:00 and these lovely women sat through many committee and budget reports.

The Women's Club is a philanthropic organization, raising money for the needs of the community, from H.I.S. House to student scholarships. Listening to the reports was fascinating. I was honored to be in the company of women who work so hard to make life better for others.

After lunch, it was time for me to stand up and address the group. I began by describing my roundabout route to becoming an author. When I was a child, I liked to make up stories, then got sidetracked by a career in software engineering before coming back to my first love. In my speech, I intended to touch on my mysteries, and end by encouraging my audience to follow their dreams, no matter how life distracts them.

A funny thing happened about halfway through my talk. Everyone seemed like they were enjoying themselves so much, I kept telling stories about my life, my books, and being an author. At last, I looked at my watch and gasped. It was 12:30, much later than I had planned to be done. These women had been there forever. They deserved to go home.

My eloquent ending was condensed to a few, rather badly-constructed sentences, but I wasn't done. A few people had questions for me. The most surprising was a request. *Could I set the murder scene of one of my books at the Round Table?*

What followed was a lively discussion of where we could put a body in the room. I was delighted. These women were even helpful at plotting mayhem.

It was finally time to end the meeting. I sold some books and donated a portion of my sales to the club, for whatever charity needed it most.

Perhaps I'm crazy to brave the terror of public speaking, but I don't feel that daring. When I speak to groups like these women, I just feel lucky.

## OUR RECREATION IS GOING TO THE DOGS

I love our Parks and Recreation Department, and dig into each Placentia Quarterly with the same gusto as when I used to read the Sears Christmas catalog. I try to sign up for at least one class a year. Sometimes I sign Dale up, too.

So far, he's been a good sport about it.

Our last class together was West Coast Swing, where we had fun learning dance steps. This year, we're taking Dog Obedience. I'm training Duffy the Corgi, and Dale is training Lady Spazzleton the Retriever-Mix.

I may have brought both dogs into our home, but Dale and Lady Spazz have bonded, as have Duffy and I, making this class a lot more competitive than when we were holding hands and triple-stepping as a couple.

When I first told Dale we were signed up, he said, "Good. Now we can prove who has the smarter dog."

We went to our first class with the dogs last Thursday, and so far it's a dead heat. Our instructor, Catherine, had given us homework for the prior week. Using a long line, we were supposed to wait until our dog was distracted, then turn and walk the opposite direction, tugging at the line. The object of this game was to get our dogs to pay attention to where we were, and learn to stay with us.

Duffy and I went dutifully to the park at the end of our street and practiced. Within two moves, he understood the game and always kept me in his view, ready to move when I did. I arrived at class feeling confident.

My confidence lasted about thirty seconds.

Corgis were bred to be all-around farm help in Wales. They guarded the home, killed vermin, and brought the cattle in at night. I might add, they did this without a lot of supervision.

From the moment we walked into the group, Duffy tried to take charge. In his little barky way, he ordered this puppy to stand there, that dog to mind his own business, etc. It was obvious that I had to take charge of him.

Being such a short dog who needs immediate correcting, my usual method of discipline is a sharp tug on the leash, along with a push with my foot to get his attention. I confess, it looks like I'm kicking him, but I swear I am not. Catherine didn't say anything, but it's possible that the other owners now think I'm evil.

Working with my bossy canine didn't give me much time to see how Dale was doing. I knew he had taken Lady Spazz out for her homework, but I didn't ask whether she was learning to follow or chasing squirrels. When I take her out for walks, I know she is easily distracted. My shoulder often hurts from being yanked in the opposite direction when she sees something interesting.

I also know she does not want to be in charge of anyone, least of all herself, and usually ignores other dogs. The glimpses I saw of her working with Dale in class looked like she was happy but clueless.

It will be a race to the finish, between my four-legged dictator and Dale's sweet simpleton, but I know we'll all have fun. Maybe next time they'll offer a Dog Obedience Dance class.

## Making plans doesn't always get things done

The other day, I was at the optometrist's office, making an appointment for a post-op checkup. I flipped through the calendar on my phone, searching for an available date and time.

"Wow, your schedule looks so busy," said the receptionist.

It might appear that way, but what she doesn't know is, half of these events will be swapped out for higher priority activities.

I think of myself as an organized person. Every day, I make plans and put them on the calendar. And every day veers from the plan. Meetings get shifted, family requests become emergencies, and even mundane tasks like bathing the dogs get rescheduled.

Being a hopeful gal, I keep adding things to the calendar that I think might happen.

This past weekend was no different. The Placentia Library Friends Foundation was hosting its annual Authors Luncheon. I've attended the luncheon for several years now, and have even been one of their "celebrity waiters." It's usually on my list of things to do.

Except this year, when I found out I had to help my horse trainer, Niki, with a group of children at a horse show. These are young girls and most of them know what to do, but I still supervise bathing the horses, check their saddles for cleanliness, and help load supplies in the truck.

Niki can't do this alone, and it's not like she can call a temp agency for a replacement.

I emailed my regrets to the PLFF president, JoAnn Sowards and replaced "Authors Luncheon" with "Horse Show" on my calendar.

Then the rains came.

No one wanted to risk a horse falling in the mud, especially with a rider, so by Tuesday, the management had decided to cancel the show. Just like that, four days of work on my calendar evaporated.

I thought about what else I could do with those hours. The house needed cleaning. I could go to a movie or read a book. Sleeping in sounded both feasible and heavenly.

It took me another day to remember the luncheon. I called the luncheon's chairperson, Ginny Sanatar. She got back to me right away, assuring me of a place somewhere at a table.

I adjusted my calendar accordingly.

The following day, I got a call from library director Jeanette Contreras.

"Could you be a celebrity waiter?"

How could I refuse? I was already going to be in the room.

The luncheon was delightful. I'm not certain what I enjoyed more, talking to old friends or meeting new ones. As a last-minute celebrity, I got to sit at a table of strangers, all from that far-away city of Fullerton. It was fun getting to know everyone and share our love of libraries.

I did my best to be a good waiter. According to my instructions, I was only supposed to serve drinks this year. Last year, I had to help serve the food. I think the staff at the Alta Vista Country Club were happy not to have so much help this year. They have, I'm sure, a system for serving the room, a system that is completely disrupted by a bunch of inexperienced pretend-waiters grabbing plates.

It all ended and we said our goodbyes. I returned home in enough time to change clothes and run out to see a movie. And I didn't even put it on my calendar.

## LEAVE THE PLANNING TO THE EXPERTS

This week, I'd like to sing the praises of a group I know well—the Placentia Library Friends Foundation. Their purpose is to support the library, both financially and through volunteer service.

The reason the PLFF is on my mind lately is that I am a member of a mystery lover's organization and we recently hosted a day honoring women mystery authors. It was much like our annual PLFF Author's Luncheon, complete with a meal. Unlike our luncheon, this event had 17 authors, and I wasn't certain I was going to survive it with my sanity intact.

This was, of course, my own fault.

Three years ago, I was on the PLFF Author's Luncheon committee. We had a big book of notes from previous years, checklists of things to do, and a calendar showing when to do them. Even with this information, there was a large group of us who met regularly to check things off according to the schedule.

It was a lot of work and yet it was easy. We knew what we had to do, assigned people to do it, and it got done. Granted, the PLFF has done this luncheon for many years, so they have learned from their experiences, but I felt safe in my role on the committee that the luncheon would be a success.

When I joined the mystery lover's organization, I volunteered to be on the board, because helping an organization is a great way to meet everyone. I really enjoy this group and have made many friends.

Last year, the president proposed an event to showcase women mystery authors, both at the local and national level. She wanted an entire day of guest speakers, panels, and lunch. I thought it sounded daunting, but the board wanted to do it and I wanted to support them.

I had experience at planning events like this. I knew how hard it could be, and what to do to make the work easier. The thing to do was to raise my hand and volunteer to lead the charge. Instead, they made me the emcee, so I sat back and waited for instructions.

This was my worst mistake.

We had meetings and things were getting done, although my internal clock kept thinking the date was approaching rapidly. Then, in January, the group made me president of the board. I was happy to take on the position, thinking the previous president would continue to work the event.

That assumption was wrong, and soon the committee was looking to me for answers. Had we gotten the grant from the national organization? How was the publicity coming along?

I should have been paying closer attention. Obviously, I rallied and we got things done. We rushed around like crazy people for the last two weeks before the event, making certain everything was in place. Two authors had to cancel due to illness, but we found replacements.

On the day of the event, it all looked polished and professional. If you didn't know about the chaos that came before, you would have thought we do this all the time. Our attendees had such a good time, they said they couldn't wait to come again next year.

I'm sure each member of our committee has a big list of "lessons learned," but there's only one item on my list. Next year we're doing it like the PLFF does it. They know how to get things done.

## SAYING GOODBYE IN OUR OWN WAY

Life on this little rock is often hard to understand. We bustle around, planning for tomorrow, yet we can be gone in a second.

I received an email on Thursday. Larry Benner, Brenda's husband, was suddenly and gravely ill. By the evening, he was gone.

Brenda is a member of the Placentia Library Friends Foundation, an active member of the Placentia Round Table Women's Club, and an all-around lovely woman.

Larry seemed to match her, step for step. I don't know if he belonged to any clubs, but each time I saw him, he was welcoming and friendly. I've only known Brenda for four years, and had met her husband at several library events. I didn't know him well, but they were the kind of couple Dale and I could have gone out to dinner with and had an interesting evening of conversation.

Now I wish we would have done that.

Instead, last Friday I went to Larry's memorial. It was a simple affair, not really a service. There was no program. No one gave a eulogy. We all just met at the Round Table, ate lunch, and shared memories. Most of the speakers were family members, but several friends gave testimony to Larry's generous spirit and endearing sense of humor.

Seeing Larry's grandchildren speak about their grandfather reminded me of losing my own. They looked to be in their teens, and I was truly impressed by their courage, to stand up in a very crowded room, maintain their composure, and talk to strangers.

I was in my 20s when my grandfather died, and I couldn't have said more than two words at his service.

My grandfather was in his 60s, and had lived his life preferring the fat to the meat. He also took up smoking when he was 10 years old, although he quit, cold turkey, when he was 63. His heart had been bothering him, so my grandmother nagged him to see the doctor. He was getting ready to go to his appointment when he had a heart attack and died.

It was my first loss and a huge shock. I kept remembering the conversation I'd had with him the prior week. It wasn't about anything important, but I remember feeling like I was an adult and Grandpa was proud of me.

As I watched Larry's grandchildren, I hoped they had such a moment with him—a few words to cherish about how much he loved them.

The memorial itself seemed appropriate. Larry was, by all accounts, a man who enjoyed time spent with others. The communal atmosphere of the occasion made me think about the times I saw him. I have a mental picture of him, sitting at a table, sideways on his chair with his right arm draped over the back, so he could talk to everyone walking past.

By contrast, my grandfather's service was traditional, held in a funeral home. It was appropriate for our family, but probably not for Grandpa. He didn't like a lot of fuss, so he would have preferred lunch with a few words said.

In the end, what matters is that these were people who were gone too soon. Their friends and family loved them, and most were lucky enough to know they were loved in return. I guess that's the only thing we need to understand as we bustle around and plan for tomorrow on this little rock.

## CONSTRUCTION DOESN'T ALWAYS STICK TO THE SCHEDULE

My horse trainer and her husband are doing some remodeling on their house. Their kitchen and dining room are currently in an uproar while floors are ripped apart and pipes are moved around. The entire process was supposed to be over in mere weeks, until the plumber went AWOL. Now, Niki just sighs when I ask her how it's going.

In an attempt at solidarity, I tell her about the light bulb I had to change, but it's not the same.

Niki's home improvement reminded me of the underpass project (or are they building a bridge?) on Kraemer Boulevard. It's been under construction for more than two years now, so when they said it would be open in May, I was skeptical.

Sure enough, we apparently had just enough rain to delay the completion date. I was told that we'd have Kraemer back in June instead.

That sounded good. To be honest, it's been closed for such a long time, I've forgotten that I used to get to Orangethorpe Avenue that way. Even my GPS navigator (I call her Wanda) has stopped trying to direct me south on Kraemer. You know it's bad when Wanda has given up.

In mid-May, I took a walk down to the construction site to see how it was going. It looked good. The bridge for the train tracks looked blockish and sturdy. The walls of the underpass were decorated with arches and columns. However…

There was no street. Some of the dirt looked flat enough to pave, but some of it still had lumps. It seemed like the center might grow up to be a median, if it ever got someone's attention.

I stood at the end and considered the date. This looked like a lot of stuff to complete within a month. Still, I figured, what do I know about construction? The closest I ever get to building anything is the furniture I buy at IKEA. At least it comes with instructions.

Last week, I found out that the underpass will be completed in July. I was not surprised. Even in May, it looked like there was a lot of concrete left to pour.

I have been wondering why the date was pushed back. The first delay was due to rain, which I understood. Granted, it was not a lot of rain, but I could see how it would pool in an underpass.

The reason for the second delay hasn't been disclosed. Unlike Niki's house, I doubt if their plumber went missing. Perhaps some other key member of the team had an emergency, or some important materials were not delivered on time. One thing I do understand about major projects is that every little piece has its place on the calendar, and one slip-up pushes everything else into the future.

I can wait until July for the grand opening. As it is, my life flies by at such warp speed, it will be July in mere moments. I hope they have a ribbon cutting ceremony. It would be fun to attend.

I'm doubting that Niki and her husband have a ceremony to celebrate their home remodel. They will probably just weep with joy when the last carpenter closes the door behind them.

This is why Dale and I limit our home improvement to changing light bulbs. We have no one to blame except ourselves if we get behind schedule.

## ASKING THE RIGHT QUESTIONS TODAY TO PREPARE FOR TOMORROW

There is a book in my shelves called "If (Questions for the Game of Life)". It has questions designed to start conversations, such as, "If you could have dinner with anyone, living or dead, who would it be?"

I was thinking about that book recently when I was asked to help our girls prepare for the Miss California competition. I consider them "our" girls in that they have grown up in Placentia and Yorba Linda and are representing our cities.

A couple of years ago, I was honored to be a judge at the local competition. Selecting young women to be the face of our city in the state, and possibly national, arena was a joyful responsibility.

I ran into Kathi Baldwin this year at the Rotary Club Cowabunga Crabfest. We chatted for a few moments before she asked if I could come to her house the next day to help give practice interviews. My week had been very long and full of activities, and I was looking forward to a day of reading the Sunday paper and relaxing.

Of course, I told her I'd be there.

Interview questions for these young women can range from asking about their education and interests to their opinions on the latest news. In many ways, the actual answer doesn't matter as much as the confidence they exude as they deliver it.

Still, it pays to know who the governor of California is. (Fortunately, all of our contestants do.)

Thinking of questions is probably as stressful as answering them. We are supposed to be grilling the girls at a lively pace. I tried to prepare by highlighting areas of each resume and making a list of current events.

Still, on Sunday mornings, my mind can be a black hole.

Two of the four girls were available, so we did our best to interview them, critique their answers, and interview them again. The girls took our notes to heart and improved each time. At the end, Kathi thanked me for my time and asked if I would be available for one more round. We compared calendars and found a Tuesday night that would work.

It was the night after I would be returning from a weekend selling books in Sacramento, then working at the ranch until 5 p.m. I knew I should really be restocking the pantry and unpacking that day, and that I would really want to be collapsing. Still, I like Kathi and believe in the organization's goals.

Of course, I told her I'd be there, with the caveat that I'd be covered in sunscreen and horse hair.

"We'll take you any way you come," she assured me.

This time, I got to interview all of the candidates. It was again, both fun and stressful, as I tried to think of topics, not interrupt the other interviewers, and take notes on the answers.

They are all such lovely young women, so earnest in their commitment to improve themselves and the world, I was torn between wanting to stand up and cheer, and needing to give them the tough critique that would help them do better. Each of them said they preferred the critique.

I have no doubt that these women, whether they win or lose, will show the rest of California the best of Placentia and Yorba Linda. And if I could have dinner with anyone, living or dead, I would have to include them, if only for their smiles.

## SHOPPING LOCALLY HAS ITS PERKS

When it comes to shopping, I like to shop locally and buy from small businesses. On the other hand, at 11 o'clock at night, Amazon is a point and click away from fulfilling my every request.

Yes, I am often a midnight shopper.

Of course, I don't buy groceries online, but I do tend to shop at the chain grocery stores. It's all about convenience. I usually need dry goods plus refrigerated ones and sometimes a few things from the freezer section. Getting them in one place is easier than making multiple trips or carrying around a cooler.

Still, I can't resist a farmers market. The rows of fresh vegetables, fruits, and nuts all call to me, saying, "You need us!" My only saving grace is that the vendors usually want cash and I usually don't carry any.

Carrying cash and having a child in college are mutually exclusive.

A couple of weeks ago, I stopped by the Placentia farmers market and could not buy anything because I had no money. The market is a small one, with only a dozen vendors or so, but still has a little of everything, and I vowed to return.

I was on a mission to buy tomatoes.

It took me a couple of weeks to remember to put a few bucks in my wallet, but once I did, I hit the market. The deliciously fresh aroma of melons, peaches, and cornhusks drew me in. I headed straight for the tomatoes. They were large and meaty, and smelled as if they'd been allowed to ripen on the vine.

In other words, they smelled like tomatoes.

I pulled a bag, maneuvered around a lady who was picking out cucumbers, and started making my selection. My first task was to figure out how many I wanted. I certainly didn't want to buy too many and have them go to waste. I decided upon three medium-sized beauties and bagged them.

The clerk was behind a display of strawberries. They were so plump and red and inviting that I had to get a container of those, too. My tomatoes weighed in slightly under the price per pound. "Go choose another tomato and you can pay the lower price," the clerk told me. I paid for my goods, while he kept reminding me to get that extra tomato.

How could I refuse? I chose another nice, fat one.

I thought I was done, until I wandered past a booth with goat cheese and kefir, which is yogurt. The man was friendly. He told me all about each product as he put each flavored chunk of cheese on a toothpick and handed it to me. Then he began to dip spoons into the kefir and tell me about each one.

The bad news is that he had such a thick accent, I think I only understood every other word. The good news is that everything he gave me was delicious. I ended up pointing at a couple of things I liked best.

Once I got home, I was able to read that I chose the goat cheese with sun-dried tomatoes and the kefir with figs. I'm not sure I could have made a bad choice.

It's been two days and I'm already half-way through everything except the kefir, and I'm trying to make that last. I shouldn't worry. The market will be back next week, and thanks to my midnight shopping, I know how to point.

## HONORING OUR CITY IS A YEARLY EVENT

I love a parade, especially when it's in Placentia on Heritage Day. It's fun to see our local bands marching down the street, interspersed among dignitaries in convertibles, and even a few horses.

For the past few years I've been lucky enough to ride in the procession. My shoulder and arm hurt for days, after all the waving, but I don't care. When I ride down Kraemer Boulevard, I get to see everyone who has come out to watch. Plus, it gives me a reason to wear my tiara.

This year, I opted for a cowboy hat with a tiara on it. The weatherman predicted a warm day and I wanted to keep the sun off my face. Plus, I didn't have to wash my hair if I put a hat on it.

Before the parade, I drove down to Tri-City Park to set up my booth. It's always a bustling place, with volunteers directing traffic and helping to unload vehicles, even in the 6 a.m. darkness. I've done this for a few years, and the directions are always the same. Be there at 6:15, even though the festival doesn't begin until 10.

Still, I like to be there at my appointed time to get my canopy raised and put my table together. It all takes less than 15 minutes and I can relax, knowing I'm ready for the day. I spend the rest of the time watching everyone else work.

The ladies in the booth next to mine were a lot of fun. As they set up their wares, one of them said, "I had lived in Placentia for years before I found out about this celebration."

I know many of my community friends are surprised by this, but I'll tell you a little secret: I didn't know about Heritage Day for years, either.

There are many reasons for this. One is that, in the pre-internet age, I confess I didn't read much of the local news. The other reason is that I used to live south of the Kraemer-Chapman corner. My routes to various locations took me west on Chapman or south on Kraemer, so I was never held up on Saturday morning by the closed parade route. I also never drove under the banner on Kraemer announcing the festival.

Clearly, I was news-deprived.

Once we moved to a street off of Alta Vista, I became aware of the celebration. Now that I drive under the banner every day, read the newspaper online, and follow Placentia's Facebook pages, I know even more.

On Saturday, I waited for Marcus to come and watch my booth while I rode in the parade. It's become a tradition for us. Since his birthday is October 12, we usually celebrate on that weekend. He drags himself from bed, hangs out at my booth, then we take him to dinner.

This year was no different. Marcus arrived, on the edge of being late, and I scampered to my post. I joined the Placentia Library car with President Al Shkoler, Trustee Jo-Anne Martin, and Clifford the Big Red Dog. The winner of the Summer Reading Celebration was also there, with her mom. Perla was a delightful girl who told me she reads a lot.

The parade was fabulous, like I knew it would be. After all, it was all part of the best day of the year—the one honoring our city.

## A LIFE OF SERVICE, WORTH REMEMBERING

I've been trying to think of a clever way to begin this column. My subject matter isn't easy to talk about. I even thought of talking about something else, but this is too important to ignore.

Last week, Placentia lost one of its dearest women.

Nancy Lone Tollefson was not a close friend of mine, in that we never visited each other's homes or spent long hours chatting. She was, however, the kind of woman who could have easily been a close friend, if either of us had ever had the time.

I met her when I joined the Placentia Library Friends Foundation. She was running the bookstore, helping with the Author's Luncheon, keeping the vending machines stocked, and doing it all with her elegant style.

When I learned of her illness, I was shocked. I had just seen her at an event. She looked a little wan, but not dangerously so. The email I received on Monday sounded grave. Cancer in her lungs, in her lymph nodes, in so many places it sounded difficult to list them all.

By Tuesday, she was gone.

The emails worried me as much as her condition. Sometimes, when emails are passed around they lose their context. By the time they got to me, they painted a picture of a very private Nancy, feeling perhaps frightened, and possibly alone.

At her memorial service, it was a comfort to know that I misunderstood.

The pews at Messiah Lutheran Church were filled with her friends and her family. From the library, there were staff members, volunteers, and trustees. The Women's Club had many representatives. And of course, a lot of her church family was there.

She might have borne her illness privately, but she was not alone.

From the service, I learned that Nancy had spent her life excelling in cooking, decorating, sewing—those activities I was taught in school back when they offered Home Economics. She even taught those skills to students. Apparently, she could have given Martha Stewart a run for her money.

Her granddaughter, her nephew, and the pastor all talked about her love for serving others. Fixing a delicious meal and presenting it at a perfectly set table was a source of joy. Helping people, whether at the library or elsewhere, was not a chore. It made her happy.

The few years I knew Nancy, she never seemed to want to step into the spotlight. She was content to accomplish any work done behind the scenes. I saw her as a woman who made quiet, firm decisions and carried them through. She didn't fuss with things.

As a woman who likes to make a choice and move on, I really appreciated that.

The other thing that struck me about Nancy was that I never saw her ruffled. She kept her cool, no matter what was happening. The pastor reported, when he saw her on that last day, she told him, “I know where I’m going.”

Clearly, Nancy was not afraid.

I’ve said this before, but it bears repeating. At a funeral once, I heard a pastor say, “You write your obituary by the life you live.” Nancy wrote of kindness, graciousness, and generosity, and it’s obvious that many people appreciated the story she told.

We’ll miss you, Nancy.

## SERVING MY COMMUNITY, ONE TASK AT A TIME

I take my job as a library trustee seriously, from being prepared at all our meetings, to attending as many community events as possible. The problem is that I also have commitments to others that interfere with my ability to be at business openings or other city events.

Every time I have to respond to an email invitation with regrets, I swear I can hear Jeanette Contreras sigh with sadness. Or maybe I'm the one sighing.

When I got the invitation to attend Ward Smith's swearing-in ceremony as Chief of Police, I cleared my calendar. I don't know Chief Smith personally, other than sitting with him at the Author's Luncheon one year, but I know what he means to this community.

I think it's amazing that we could have this homegrown police chief. In my youth, I was bored and unimpressed by my hometown, and left as soon as I could. Although I love Placentia and wouldn't want to live anywhere else, I now realize that my impatience to leave had more to do with me than the city.

Apparently, Ward knew a good town when he saw it. He stayed in Placentia.

The ceremony was outside, in the civic center courtyard, on a beautiful afternoon. Every chair was occupied, and more people stood around the back. I sat next to Rosalina Davis, of Tlaquepaque, so I was in good company.

A number of people spoke highly of the new chief and his many accomplishments. I never knew Chief Smith was the first K-9 officer in Placentia. No wonder I like him so much—it's hard not to trust a guy who likes dogs.

Retired chief Rick Hicks was particularly inspiring, comparing Smith to a quote from Elbert Hubbard: "Some men succeed by what they know, some by what they do, and a few by what they are."

By the time City Administrator Troy Butzlaff administered the oath, I think everyone was ready to throw confetti and dance.

Chief Hicks and I had enjoyed a nice friendship. Writing mysteries based in Placentia means I often have questions for law enforcement. Every time I approached him with the words, "Hypothetically speaking," he laughed.

After Chief Smith's ceremony, the line to congratulate him was across the square, so I thought I'd wait for a quieter time to add my two cents. Instead, I spoke with Kathi Baldwin, who was looking for volunteers to help as ushers at the Miss Placentia Scholarship Pageant.

By the time I had offered my help, I turned to see that the line had disappeared.

"Congratulations, Chief Smith," I said as I shook his hand.

Smiling and gracious, he thanked me.

"I kind of bugged your predecessor with questions about law enforcement," I warned him. "I may have questions for you from time to time."

He was still smiling. "Oh, that's all right. That's what I'm here for."

I thanked him, then added, "Just know, any question I ask is purely hypothetical."

The chief laughed, but we'll see if he's still laughing when I ask him one of my more macabre questions.

I left the civic center feeling glad that I attended. Not only did I get to be a part of our community's welcome to our new chief and old friend, I got another chance to be of service, via Kathy Baldwin.

Being an usher is the least I can do for my town.

## THERE'S ALWAYS AN OPPORTUNITY TO VOLUNTEER

Being a volunteer is a rewarding experience. When I give to others, I get joy in return. Who doesn't love that feeling of being useful?

I wasn't always a volunteer. In high school, my passion for ecology ran high, so when I wasn't cleaning up the environment on Earth Day, I was bugging my principal to let me organize a school clean-up day.

He never let me do it, by the way. I wonder if he regrets that decision.

After high school, it felt like I was so busy scrambling around trying to be an adult, my view of the world narrowed. Perhaps it's the same for most 18-25 year olds. Just before our empathy blooms, we have one more round of self-centeredness.

I've since volunteered at church, at Marcus' schools, and of course, at the library. The library was actually waiting for me. I think they contacted me the week after Marcus graduated, to see if I'd like to help.

The rest is history.

Recently, I attended the annual Author's Luncheon, held at the Alta Vista Country Club by the Placentia Library Friends Foundation. It is their largest fundraiser of the year, and the money raised goes to many programs, from children to adults. Having served on this committee, I know how much work goes into making the event successful.

This year's event was stellar. Two authors, D.P. (Doug) Lyle and Jan Burke presented a lively session of questions and answers from the audience. I happen to know Doug and Jan, so it was fun to chat with them, and to watch them entertain the crowd.

And what a crowd it was. The room looked packed and felt like it was vibrating with high energy.

I was asked to be a celebrity waiter again, and was happy to do so, although my fellow celebrities made me feel particularly un-famous. Who can compete with Ward Smith, Connie Underhill, or Scott Nelson?

My table was filled with interesting people. Everyone talked about who had lived in Placentia the longest, and where they went to school. I sat next to a fascinating woman who had been a probation officer. We discussed her job and why she retired, along with other topics.

One of the nicest things she told me was that the Placentia Library has the best collection of audio books of any library in Orange County.

"I don't have time to sit and read, but I can put on a book while I work or drive and listen to the story," she said. "The Los Angeles library is good, too, but our library is the best."

I was happily surprised to hear this, and could only guess it's because, as a special district, we are an independent entity and can choose our distributors for audio books and ebooks that give our patrons the most options.

At the end of the luncheon, I would have gladly stayed and chatted more, but it was time to run off to the next thing on my to-do list: cleaning my house. I've got a friend visiting next week and I want to provide fresh towels, clean sheets, and fur-free furniture.

You could say I'm volunteering a bedroom. It's just one more way I can give to someone else and get a smile on my face in return.

## CULTIVATING A PASSION FOR WRITING IS MY PASSION

Marcus inherited many traits from his parents, both physical and otherwise. One thing he got from both sides was our passion for what we do. He has been pursuing music since he was 7, when he asked for guitar lessons, and will soon graduate from college with a bachelor's degree in music, double-majoring in vocal jazz studies and composition.

It's the best trait we could have passed down to our son, and the one thing I would wish for all people.

This week, I got to see a room full of children who showed me that same passion, only the object of their desire was the one closest to my own heart: writing. I was invited to speak at Golden Elementary School, where teacher Jenner Rasic has been leading a group of 6th graders in an exercise to write their own novels.

In the writer community, there is an event called National Novel Writing Month, or "NaNoWriMo." Writers sign up and attempt to write 50,000 words within 30 days. It's fun and exhausting.

The 15 children of Golden volunteered to try this, although Mrs. Rasic set the goal a little lower, to 2,000 words. Still, I was impressed as one girl told me that she had written 9,000, and one of the boys had written 30,000. That's a lot of words.

I was invited to their class to discuss the editing process. Although I've worked with young people before, my previous experience with a group of children is when I taught the now-retired "Art Docent" series for Marcus' class, from 2nd through 4th grade. I prepared 30 minutes of lecture and 30 minutes of activity.

What I didn't realize is that I could not slow down or pause without losing the kids' attention. I delivered a half-hour's lecture in 10 minutes. Good thing they loved the activity.

I was met at Golden by two of the students in the class. They were formal and polite as they introduced themselves. As we walked out the door, the young man pointed to his partner and said, "She's supposed to dump me at the lunch line, then take you to Mrs. Rasic's class."

"Dump you?" I asked. "That sounds so harsh. Can't she drop you off gently?"

That seemed to relax them both as they laughed.

It turns out, I didn't have to worry about keeping their attention. I had a room full of enrapt listeners, 15 young men and women, excited to hear how to look at their words on the page and make them better.

Mrs. Rasic was pretty thrilled, too. Each time I told the children something about the editing process, she'd smile and say, "We were just talking about how to do that."

My only complaint was that my time with them ended too soon. Forty-five minutes seemed to fly at sonic speed. To thank them for their invitation, I gave them all a copy of my horse's memoir, autographed by Snoopy himself. The looks on their faces filled my heart.

Sometimes I complain about my busy schedule, but I will travel to just about any location to talk to children who are passionate about writing. I think a curious mind and a passion for something are the best resources for living a full life.

## GOOD HEALTH REQUIRES A LITTLE WORK

We all know that regular exercise and healthy eating are good for us. They help us live longer and feel better. Although, I would argue that chocolate cake makes me happy, which keeps me emotionally healthy.

Too bad the bathroom scale disagrees with me.

I was indulgent last year, eating food that pleased me and exercising sporadically. Blame it on age. I turned 60 and decided to treat myself to a year of fun. That meant sticky toffee pudding in Scotland, caramel cheesecake at home, and a general avoidance of the scale.

My horse was making it obvious that I weighed more each time I got into the saddle. I'm sure if he could talk, he'd have asked me to get off and come back when I was alone.

By January, I knew I needed to rein in my bad habits, and take care of my health.

I've already had my colonoscopy and my mammogram, and have scheduled my yearly checkup for next week. All I need is a dermatologist and I'm set for the year, medically speaking.

My diet has been re-focused on whole grains, lean meat, and more vegetables. I've also begun using my app that shows the nutritional value of just about every food in the world. It lets me see that the Panera cupcake I'd like to eat will have to replace my lunch and dinner if I'm going to get my jeans zipped without lying on the bed.

As for exercise, apart from riding my horses and walking the dogs, I realized I needed to do something else. I've always wanted to try yoga, for two reasons. One is that I've never been very flexible and I'd like to touch my toes someday. The other reason is that I have a high energy mind and a low energy body.

It would be nice if they got along better.

I found a lovely yoga studio in Placentia, and spoke with the owner to see what kind of class would best suit my old, stiff bones. She recommended quite a few options. Lucky for me, they were offering a deal to newcomers. Unlimited classes for two months. There were at least six classes each week that I could choose from.

I could yoga myself into a frenzy until March.

After my first class, I rethought that idea. Yoga is not supposed to hurt, and the instructor/owner Debbie was good at reminding us not to strain our muscles or push them beyond their limits. It was more important to keep the movements flowing, the energy level up, and our breathing consistent.

My low energy body understood this, but my high energy mind is such an overachiever, it wanted to keep up with everything Debbie was doing. She told us often that we should only do what was comfortable.

Instead, I did more.

By the end of the first class, I felt tired, but good. I got into my car and drove home. As I stepped toward the front door, my legs wobbled like overcooked pasta. I managed to get into the house, where I collapsed into a chair.

Over the next few classes, I learned to tell my high energy mind to shut up.

It's nice to be back in the swing of good health. I definitely feel better, and have more energy. Of course, I'd feel a lot happier if I had some chocolate cake.

## Strolling Down Memory Lane with the Placentia Quarterly

I'm trying to reduce the amount of mail that comes into my house. It's been harder than I thought. Even though I sign up for paperless billing and do a lot of shopping online, I still get mail from my bank offering me services and catalogs from the stores I frequent.

Perhaps we are not on the same page, ecology-wise.

The one piece of mail I enjoy getting is the Placentia Quarterly. It's always full of promise. I could learn to dance the tango, teach the dogs to catch a Frisbee, or take a group excursion to somewhere fun.

Dale and I have actually taken some of these classes. We learned to dance West Coast Swing, although my prior training in the Lindy Hop made my hips swing a little too much.

We also took the dogs to an obedience class, with mixed results. Duffy now has a few more commands to ignore, but Lady Spazzleton decreased her time between "Sit" and actually sitting by at least 30 seconds.

I was happy to receive the newsletter this week. This quarter is all about summer camps for the kids. I remember those days, when Dale and I were working parents and Marcus needed to be somewhere during the daytime. Every spring, I combed through the quarterly, flyers at school, and any other resource I could find, looking for camps.

Marcus went to camps for science, art, basketball, soccer, roller hockey, and maybe more things I can't remember. All I recall are the Excel spreadsheets I made to keep track of where he was, when, and how much it was costing to be there. I also have a dim memory of all the time-juggling Dale and I did to get him to the camp by 9 a.m. and pick him up at 4 p.m. and still work our 8-hour days.

Some camps were repeated for a couple of years. Cal State Fullerton's art camp was one of them, mostly because it was two weeks long. Going to the same place at the same time for two weeks was blissful.

I asked Marcus if he remembered going to those camps. He told me he remembered the science camps and the Chapman University basketball camp. That fascinated me, since I thought those one-week science camps flew by at warp speed.

"Oh, and that art camp," he added.

"We still have your artwork all over the house," I said.

"Yes, I have noticed."

My mom radar detected a note of embarrassment, so like any other good mother, I decided to tease him about it.

"Someday when you're famous, I'm going to give tours of our house and point to your paintings and tell everyone that you were creative at anything you touched."

He took it in good stride. "And I'll be like, 'no, mom, just don't.'"

Okay, I really wouldn't, if only because I'd have to keep my house too clean for that.

I went back to the newsletter to see if there were any new classes. Perhaps we could learn a martial art, or brush up our tennis skills. The ad for the Rotary Club's Cowabunga reminded me to buy my tickets.

If nothing else, the quarterly lets me know where I can take my papers to be shredded. I'll be shredding everything except the quarterly.

## WALKING TO THE BEAT IS MORE FUN WITH FRIENDS

Getting older has its pros and cons. Time isn't always good to your body or your mind, but naps are fashionable again. And, as they say, considering the alternative, it's good to grow older.

One of the nicer things I'm finding is that I'm not as concerned about what others think. Sing a solo? Sure. Dress up as a Viking? No problem. Wear a tiara to high tea? If the Queen can, so can I.

Recently, I saw a video of a man on a busy street in New York City. He was promoting a new type of exercise. There was music blasting, and he was dancing as he walked down the street, encouraging other people to join him. The video called it dance-walking, and I was impressed.

That guy was busting some moves.

I shared the video on my social media page, along with the comment that I'd do this with a group of my crazy friends. I should have known one of my friends would be just that crazy.

Jeanette Contreras, Placentia Library director, is well known for her love of fun and whimsy. She entertains the audience at the Author's Luncheon every year, has spearheaded many family events at the library, and encourages the staff to find ways to engage our community.

"Great! When do we start?" she commented on my page.

We got the details worked out. She would bring a mini-speaker if I would supply the music. Wednesday worked best for both of us.

"Kraemer Boulevard or All America Way," she asked, when we were contemplating our route.

"Let's start on All America Way," I said. "There's less traffic to stop with our dancing skills."

We decided on a dance-walk of 15-30 minutes. I picked out 30 minutes of perky music. At home, I played each tune to make certain it was danceable, moving through the house with some steps I'd try on the street. I was a little dismayed to find that after one song, I was fairly out of breath.

Jeanette is far younger than me. If I didn't pace myself, she'd be dragging me back to the library after 5 minutes.

On Wednesday afternoon, I met Jeanette on the street. We plugged in the mini-speaker, cranked up the tunes, and started dancing. Well, okay, we were mostly walking, but our arms were dancing.

We didn't see many people on our route. Jeanette said our business manager offered to video our outing, but she declined. I suppose people might have taken some photos of us from their windows. It doesn't matter to me, although I do wish my moves were less silly and more coordinated.

After 15 minutes, we were back at the library. For our first outing, that was long enough.

I'd call our dance-walking a success, although we need to adjust a few things. The mini-speaker was not loud enough, forcing us to stay close. And of course, with only two of us, we talked… a lot. The amount of chatter meant we downsized our dance moves to save our breath.

We are planning to do this every Wednesday at 1:30. More people would make it more fun, so we're going to be seeking volunteers who want to get a little exercise.

Want to dance down the street with us? It feels great, and trust me, no one's watching. At least, no one that we could see.

## ABOUT THE AUTHOR

Gayle Carline is a typical Californian, meaning she was born somewhere else. She moved to Orange County from Illinois in 1978, and landed in Placentia a few years later.

Her husband, Dale, bought her a laptop for Christmas in 1999 because she wanted to write. A year after that, he gave her horseback riding lessons. When she bought her first horse, she finally started writing.

Gayle soon became a regular contributor to California Riding Magazine, and in March, 2005, she began writing a humor column for her local newspaper, the Placentia News-Times. Every week, she entertains readers with stories of her life with Dale and their son, Marcus.

Believing she should experience reincarnation while she is still alive, Gayle has been a software engineer, a dancer, and even a flying angel for the Crystal Cathedral's Glory of Christmas.

In her spare time, Gayle likes to sit down with friends and laugh over a glass of wine. Or two.

For more merriment, visit her at **http://www.gaylecarline.com**.

## ALSO BY THIS AUTHOR

Freezer Burn (A Peri Minneopa Mystery)
Hit or Missus (A Peri Minneopa Mystery)
The Hot Mess (A Peri Minneopa Mystery)
Clean Sweep (A Peri Minneopa Short Story)

Murder on the Hoof

From the Horse's Mouth: One Lucky Memoir

What Would Erma Do? Confessions of a First Time Humor Columnist
Are You There, Erma? It's Me Gayle
Raising the Perfect Family and Other Tall Tales
Holly Jolly Holidays

www.ingramcontent.com/pod-product-compliance
Lightning Source LLC
LaVergne TN
LVHW051402080426
835508LV00022B/2939

*9781943654024*